Quarterly Essay

Quarterly Essay is published four times a year by Black Inc., an imprint of Schwartz Books Pty Ltd. Publisher: Morry Schwartz.

ISBN 9781760645007 ISSN 1444-884x

Subscriptions – 1 year print & digital (4 issues): $99.99 within Australia incl. GST. Outside Australia $134.99. 1 year digital only: $64.99.

Payment may be made by Mastercard or Visa, or by cheque made out to Schwartz Books. Payment includes postage and handling.

To subscribe, fill out and post the subscription card or form inside this issue, or subscribe online:

quarterlyessay.com
subscribe@quarterlyessay.com
Phone: 61 3 9486 0288

Correspondence should be addressed to:

The Editor, Quarterly Essay
22–24 Northumberland Street
Collingwood VIC 3066 Australia
Phone: 61 3 9486 0288 / Fax: 61 3 9011 6106
Email: quarterlyessay@blackincbooks.com

Editor: Chris Feik. Management: Elisabeth Young. Publicity: Anna Lensky. Design: Guy Mirabella. Associate Editor: Kirstie Innes-Will. Production Coordinator: Marilyn de Castro. Typesetting: Typography Studio.

Printed in Australia by McPherson's Printing Group. The paper used to produce this book comes from wood grown in sustainable forests.

HARD NEW WORLD

Our Post-American Future

Hugh White

A quarter of a century ago, the world was a pretty comfortable place for Australia. Our prosperity seemed assured by the apparently irresistible and irreversible forces of globalisation, driven by free trade and the free movement of investment, technology, ideas and people. That in turn was turbo-charging our Asian neighbours, especially China, offering us economic opportunities that were the envy of the world. Our security seemed assured by the apparently unchallengeable power of the United States, its manifest determination to uphold a global order in which aggression would be swiftly and surely punished, and its deep commitment to close allies, of which we were among the closest. The values that we like to think define us – our commitment to electoral democracy, the rule of law, freedom of speech, respect for human rights, tolerance of diversity – were now, we thought, becoming truly universal, as the long arc of world history bent towards freedom and justice. All this – what our political leaders have in mind when they talk about the "rules-based order" – was thanks to America. Australia was flourishing in a world made safe and easy for us by American power, influence and ideas.

Since then, a lot has gone wrong: 9/11 and the War on Terror, the global financial crisis, the Covid-19 pandemic and the fractious and faltering struggle against global warming, to name just the most obvious. And now we seem to face something even more fundamental: a shift from a world which worked well for us to one that looks a lot harder to navigate. The basis of our prosperity is imperilled by the collapse of globalisation and the prospect that rival trade blocs will be built on its ruins. The foundation of our security is undermined by the eclipse of the US-led rules-based order. And the power of our values is undermined by the persistence of strong authoritarian governments in many powerful states, and the rise of populism and the erosion of democratic norms in places where these once seemed strongest, especially the United States. The world America made for us is passing away. Its place is being taken by a new and harder post-American world, and we are at a loss to know what to make of it and how to make our way in it. Our leaders are still in denial about all this. They hope that the old rules-based order will somehow revive and survive so that things go back to the way they were in John Howard's day.

They grew complacent when the shock of Trump's first term gave way to the misleading normality of the Biden presidency, which somewhat restored confidence in democratic values and institutions. They were reassured too by Washington's apparently robust response to the Russian invasion of Ukraine, while its commitment to resisting China and upholding our nation's security seemed to be reaffirmed by AUKUS.

But now Trump is back, worse than ever. His first months back in office have been an astonishing spectacle. His absurdly inappropriate appointments to key jobs. His grotesque ideas on Gaza. His open contempt for US allies. His threats to Canada, Panama and Greenland. His treatment of Ukraine. His frontal assault on the global trading system. The wrecking ball he has swung at the machinery of US government. His contempt for democracy and the rule of law. We must now recognise that Trump and the movement he inspires constitute a decisive shift in the way America works and in how this shapes the world. We must now see just how much we have *already* lost of the old world order, and how much more we are in danger of losing.

But the can't-look-away spectacle of Trump's second presidency should not mislead us. Everything that is happening is not just because of Trump. Deeper forces are also at work, and we must understand them if we are to understand this hard new world and how to make our way in it. That is what this essay is about. It focuses especially on the strategic elements of the current crisis. Ever since Imperial Japan destroyed Britain's position in Asia almost eighty-four years ago, our security and our place in the international system have been built upon our dependence on America, formalised seventy-four years ago in the ANZUS Treaty. Now that long era is ending, and we come face to face with our post-American future.

We are not alone. US allies in Europe and Asia have also relied on America, but they are now thinking seriously about their post-American futures. We have not even started. In February, as the full extent of Trump's abandonment of Europe over Ukraine was becoming clear, Anthony Albanese blithely confirmed that he believed our alliance with the United States was "rock solid." Peter Dutton was equally confident. Our alliance, we are told, stands above the ebb and flow of politics and policies in either country. Presidents may come and go, but nothing can shake the sure foundations of this great partnership.

America has strategic alliances with a lot of countries – over fifty, by one count. But the custodians of Australia's alliance with America – political leaders, officials, commentators and assorted schmoozers – believe that ours is something very special. They are convinced that between Australia and America there is a unique intimacy and mutual commitment that lifts our alliance under the ANZUS Treaty to a different level, above the cool and sometimes cynical calculus of national interests where ordinary alliances operate. Faced with the prospect of a second Trump presidency, Penny Wong said last year that the US–Australia relationship "is bigger than the events of the day" and is "shaped by enduring friendship and timeless values."

The claim is that we are more than allies, we are "mates." Tony Abbott once went so far as to tell an audience in Washington that Australians did not really regard America as a foreign country. "We are more than allies, we're family," he said. Thus the proud boast that Australia has fought alongside America in every war it has fought since 1900. How else to explain America's generosity in letting us share its most prized military assets under AUKUS?

This is an illusion, and like many illusions it springs from anxiety. We are eager to claim that the alliance is built on foundations firmer than the shifting sands of national policies and interests precisely because we are unsure that policy and interests alone are enough to keep it alive. For all the sentimental talk of imperishable bonds, Australians have always been the most anxious of allies, and for good reason. No country in history has depended so much, and for so long, on allies so far away from us and to whom we matter so little for the defence of their most vital interests.

That is why for 150 years, since the splendour of Pax Britannica first began to fray, "Can we depend on our allies?" has always been one of the central questions of our national life. And what we have learnt, again and again, is that all alliances, without exception, are transactional. That is what we discovered when Singapore fell in 1942, when the vaunted imperial ties of history, language, values and kinship were outweighed by the demands of Britain's own vital interests.

It was a lesson imprinted indelibly on the minds of the wartime and postwar generations, for whom the Fall of Singapore was a touchstone, reinforced by Britain's final withdrawal east of Suez after 1968 and America's uncertain support in regional crises of the early 1960s. But the lesson needs relearning today, as we emerge from the era we still call the "post–Cold War," when American power and resolve appeared to be limitless and unchallenged – rather like Britain's seemed at the height of its nineteenth-century imperial power. In a world with only one global power, an alliance with that power seemed to offer all we needed to make our way in the world. That era has now passed.

Recognising this and adapting to it is especially hard because the flipside of our deep comfort with the world America has made for us has always been a certain ambivalence about Australia's embrace of an alternative, Asian destiny. That has offered opportunities for politicians to exploit if they dare. John Howard was one who did. His mantra was that Australia does not have to choose between its history and its geography, by which he meant that we can bow to the logic of geography and comparative advantage by building our economy on Asian markets, but still look to America and Europe for our identity and our security. Australians would feel, he used to say, more "relaxed and comfortable" that way.

It seemed to work in the 1990s, when America's power seemed unchallengeable, and it was possible to think that Asia need be no more to us than a market for our exports. It made less sense by the time Howard left office in 2007, as I think he may have understood, because by then Asia was already more than just a market for us. But it didn't work for Scott Morrison and Peter Dutton in 2020 and 2021. They tried to make political hay from Australians' growing anxiety about China's power and ambition by talking up the China threat and accusing their opponents of being agents of Beijing. Their David and Goliath act played well for a time, but not so much in the 2022 election, when Chinese Australian voters deserted the Coalition in numbers sufficient to cost them a couple of seats. For an electorally significant number of Australians today, Asia is not just a market: it is where they come from, and it means a lot to them. A lot more of us may be starting to understand, with or without Trump's help, the truth of Paul Keating's mantra that Australia must look for its security in Asia, not from Asia.

AMERICAN REVOLUTION

It is hard to forget what we saw unfold in the Oval Office on 28 February 2025, when Donald Trump and his vice president, J.D. Vance, confronted Ukraine's President Volodymyr Zelenskyy in front of the TV cameras. It was certainly one of the most remarkable and disturbing diplomatic encounters ever filmed. Trump, back in the presidency for a second time, was somehow both more in control and more out of control than ever.

There was something disconcertingly raw about that encounter, in the way Trump revealed himself with such relish. Narcissistic, cruel and avaricious. Irrepressible, unfiltered and unfettered. Compulsively transgressive and heretical. Almost hormonally drawn to strength and arrogance in others, while being repelled by anything suggesting modesty, weakness or vulnerability. Of course, we have been seeing all this for nearly a decade, ever since Trump began his assault on the US political system in 2016. But the scene in the Oval Office that day struck deeper. Trump and his sidekick, two powerful men in very comfortable positions, facing no very tough decisions, took pleasure together in bullying and humiliating a third man, who, cornered like his country and in peril, faced one of the toughest decisions any person could face.

History will judge how far President Zelenskyy deserves his reputation as a hero and an inspiration, and its verdict will be complex. But there is no doubt that he, and through him the country he leads and represents, deserved respect and deep sympathy. As he confronted his tormentors that day, he carried a terrible burden. He had to find a way to end a war he could not win against an enemy he cannot escape. For three years he had shown courage and skill in rallying his country to fight. Now he had to show even greater courage and skill in leading them to understand that there would be no victory, and to accept instead a perilous and probably temporary peace.

This is the person who America's leaders, Trump and Vance – because, yes, there are *two* of them now – goaded, hectored and humiliated in the Oval Office that day. They did it for no better reason than to show how tough they think they are. And for them it *was* just a show. "This is going to be great television," was Trump's breathtakingly flippant, cruel and revealing remark at the end. To carry on like that in the presence of a man bearing Ukraine's burdens showed a lack of common humanity that is, in truth, sociopathic: "a mental health condition in which a person consistently shows no regard for right and wrong and ignores the rights and feelings of others."

Over time, with endless repetition, Trump's transgressions become familiar and cease to shock. But it is important if we are to understand the world we live in not to lose our sense of bewilderment and dismay that this person leads, inspires and controls – indeed, constitutes – a political movement which has seized the key instruments of national power in America and to which the US political system has, it seems, no effective response. He defies all that we thought we knew about that system, and indeed about the whole way electoral democracies work around the world. Is there any precedent at any time for a person like Trump being elected and re-elected anywhere in any functioning democracy? Perhaps the closest precedent is Italy's Silvio Berlusconi, but he pales beside Trump. Berlusconi proved to be little more than an ageing party animal. Donald Trump is leading a revolution.

Trump defies so completely our ideas of what political leaders are and how they behave that even now it can be hard to judge his significance. It is a cliché that Trump's opponents made the mistake of taking him literally but not seriously, whereas the right way to take him was seriously but not literally. Now that advice seems out of date. We need to take him literally *and* seriously.

Taking Trump literally means recognising that what he offers Americans is nothing less than a revolution in the way the United States is governed and the way it relates to the rest of the world. Taking him seriously means recognising that he seems to be in a position to achieve that revolution. Above all, he has a mandate from the US electorate. Last year, Americans right across the country – people who knew what he'd done in his first term, knew how he'd acted when he lost in 2020 and knew what he said during the 2024 campaign about what he would do if he won again – voted for him in unprecedented numbers. It seems the more Americans know about Trump, they more they vote for him.

Apparently, it does not matter that the revolution he offers has no coherent objective and that it is conjured entirely from myths and prejudices, with his own personality the only credo. That seems to be the revolution that most Americans want, or think they want, which tells us how deeply they reject the old American political order. That can only mean that deep forces are at work, economic and social trends which over decades have undermined so many Americans' confidence in and commitment to the old vision of America that for so long underpinned the policies of both parties and the constitutional order within which they worked.

And it is not just the voters. In 2025 other centres of power and influence have lined up with Trump in his second term in a way that was unthinkable in his first. By crowding into his inauguration, the tech titans – men who stand at the apex of America's economy, and hence of its society – provided an endorsement of his revolutionary mandate almost as potent as the election result itself.

It nonetheless still seems incredible that the foundational principles of American government, enshrined in a constitution which, we thought, is revered by Americans to a degree incomprehensible to citizens of other constitutional democracies, should prove so vulnerable to Trump's assaults. Plainly, it shows that Trump has some extraordinary talents. But equally it shows the weakness of the political system and institutions that he has subjugated, starting with America's two great political parties.

What does it tell us about the Republican Party that a man like Trump, with no political experience, no political base, no political program and what seemed like insurmountable political liabilities could defy the party's leadership to seize its presidential nomination in 2016? What does it tell us that today, after all that has happened, the party is even more abjectly subordinated to Trump's will and whims? Trump may be formidable, but the Republican Party didn't put up much of a fight. That may be in part because the pattern of Republican politics that created Trump has deep roots in the

GOP, back to Barry Goldwater in the early 1960s, Nixon's Southern Strategy in the late '60s and early '70s, the rise of Reagan in the '70s and '80s, Rush Limbaugh, Pat Buchanan and Newt Gingrich in the '90s, and the Tea Party movement that formed under and against Obama.

Trump's rise raises big question about the Democrats too. How could the party of FDR, JFK and, yes, Bill Clinton have so little to offer American voters that so many of them have turned in preference to Donald Trump and so many more could not be bothered to turn out to vote to defeat him? How to explain or excuse the debacle of the 2024 Democratic presidential campaign, when the party hierarchy inexplicably acquiesced in Biden's unconscionable bid for a second term? And where is the evidence now that the Democrats have any coherent ideas to offer US voters as an alternative to Trump's revolution, any plan to defend the vital pillars of the US constitutional order from him, or anyone who looks like they can win back the White House in 2028?

We do not know how resilient and robust the other institutions of American government will prove to be in resisting and containing Trump's revolution. But we can say that ever since the Trump era began in 2016, most of us have consistently overestimated the capacity of those institutions to contain him. The Congress, the courts, the bureaucracy, the states and the media have all been unable to stop his assault on the American state and its constitution. We can see where this could lead by looking ahead to the 2028 presidential election. Even if Trump does not defy the constitution to seek a third term, his movement will surely try to overturn the result unless his anointed successor is elected. They were prepared to do that in 2020 and 2024. How much better prepared and more determined will they be in 2028? What are the chances, then, that Trump's mysterious and momentous conquest of the American political system will be defeated at the ballot box? It is an extraordinary fate to befall what was one of the most robust and successful political systems the world has ever seen.

What does that mean for US foreign policy? Despite Trump's radically disruptive instincts, the key elements of US foreign and defence policy emerged from his first term largely unscathed. Credit for that belongs partly to Congressional Republicans, steeped in the bipartisan orthodoxies of US global leadership, who then still had the resolve to block many of his more radical proposals. Even more credit may belong to Trump's own officials, including many of his most senior subordinates. Steeped in the same orthodoxies, they circumvented or simply ignored presidential whims they disagreed with. That is why when Joe Biden took over he found it easy to blithely reassure US allies that "America is back." It helped that this was what those allies desperately wanted to hear.

But this time is different. Back in 2016, Trump and his supporters hardly expected to win. They had no idea how to build an administration and only the vaguest idea of what they wanted it to do. Lacking a cadre of Trump true believers, they had no alternative but to fill key positions with traditional Republicans who had no real commitment to Trump and whose more orthodox views on foreign and defence policy were very different from his. This time the Trump team did expect to win, and they were fully prepared. They seem to have recruited a host of people who are dedicated to Donald Trump and his vision of America's place in the world.

This is most strikingly true of his most senior officials. We have seen a remarkable cavalcade of deplorably unsuitable people appointed and confirmed to important positions, including Pete Hegseth as secretary of defence, Tulsi Gabbard as intelligence chief, and Robert Kennedy as secretary of health. But consider too the more substantial members of the new Trump administration. Compare Trump's first vice president, Mike Pence, with J.D. Vance, or Marco Rubio with Trump's previous secretary of state, Mike Pompeo. Pence and Pompeo were traditional Republicans with an unquestioned commitment to the boilerplate orthodoxies of US global leadership.

Pence would never have spoken of Europe to the Europeans in the way Vance did at the Munich Security Conference in February this year, and he would never have ganged up with Trump to bully Zelenskyy. Pompeo would never have spoken of America as one great power among others in a multipolar global order in the way Rubio has done (we will come back to this below). This time Trump is surrounded by people dedicated to his worldview and committed to reshaping America, and America's place in the world, to accord with it. It seems only prudent for other countries, including Australia, to expect that they will succeed, and start planning accordingly.

*

That scene in the Oval Office with Zelenskyy perfectly exemplified Trump's vision of America in the world. He rejects the whole idea of America as the global leader, upholding and enforcing international order and promoting American values for the good of the world as a whole. To Trump, America's sole purpose in the world is to protect America's direct interests in its own security and prosperity. And it is clear to him what that does and does not require. America's security does not require it to defend countries far from America, because it is protected by two "big, beautiful oceans" that surround the Western Hemisphere, and what happens on the other side of those oceans does not really matter much to America's security. Thanks to those big, beautiful oceans, he said, the war in Ukraine is "far more important to Europe than it is to us." What really matters for American security is what happens on America's side of those oceans – in the Western Hemisphere. There America must be in complete control – hence Trump's extraordinary obsessions with Greenland, Panama and Canada.

Nor does he think that America's prosperity requires deep engagement with or commitment to other countries. He believes that the multilateral global trading system, designed and maintained by Washington since 1945 to promote free trade, is bad for America. He seems to see international trade as a source of weakness, not strength, so he wants America to be as self-sufficient as possible. And he thinks that when America does trade, it should do so through bilateral deals in which he can drive hard bargains to disproportionally benefit America at others' expense – or so he imagines.

This is a revolutionary vision. It directly repudiates the conception of America's place in the world that has been debated, refined and celebrated by generations of American politicians, officials, scholars and journalists, supported by generations of US voters, and sustained with huge commitments of treasure and blood. No wonder so many people in America and beyond – including in Canberra – find it so hard to accept that Trump really means to abandon the old vision, or that the American political system and the American people will let him abandon it.

Might they be right? It is perhaps too early to say how far Trump's revolution will go in transforming America's place in the global trading system. His "Liberation Day" tariff shock certainly suggested the scale of his ambitions. What he announced that day was the most radical attack on free trade since the early 1930s. But it also revealed the forces arrayed against him. They include internal contradictions within the policy itself, driven by conflicting ideas of what it is supposed to achieve. Some of Trump's most senior economic officials, including Stephen Miran, chair of Trump's Council of Economic Advisers, and Scott Bessent, secretary to the Treasury, have spoken of using the tariff shock to compel countries, especially US allies, to join a Washington-led trade bloc to exclude and isolate China and accept new trade and currency arrangements favourable to America. Those who do not comply will not just suffer high tariffs but lose American strategic protection as well. Others seem to hope that the threat of such a bloc, and the sky-high tariffs already imposed on China, will force Beijing to negotiate a comprehensive new trade deal favourable to America, and once that's done things will go back to something like normal. A third view is that the tariffs are simply intended to shield America's economy from imports, from China or anywhere else, and raise revenue: in which case there will be no tariff-cutting deals with China or anyone else. No one knows which of these outcomes Trump himself wants: he probably finds all three options appealing in different ways, but obviously they are mutually incompatible. That is a big problem.

But economic and commercial realities pose an even bigger problem for the trade policy side of Trump's revolution. The bond market soon made Trump step back from much of what he announced on Liberation Day. The dire consequences for key US industries and consumers forced further concessions, and may well force more. Trump's negotiators will find that their bargaining position with other countries is much weaker than they imagined, especially with US allies and with China, because America is simply not that important to most of them as a trade partner. It will become clear that making iPhones in America defies economic logic and common sense. It may well be that Trump will eventually abandon most of what he announced on Liberation Day, while no doubt claiming a brilliant success. The reality is that Trump's trade policies run directly counter to America's economic interests, and not even Trump can swim far against that tide. Trump's trade policies will have lasting consequences and do a lot of damage, but the global trading order will not be permanently transformed by his revolution.

But the strategic dimension of Trump's revolution is different. His vision of America's place in the global strategic order swims with the tide of history, not against it, and it fits America's circumstances today better than the old orthodoxies of US global leadership. That is because the world has changed a lot since the 1940s, and especially since the end of the Cold War.

Donald Trump's critics often say that he is taking America back to the isolationism of the nineteenth century, which they assume is a bad thing. But something like the old isolationism makes sense for America today, and to see why, it helps to look at why it made sense for over a century from George Washington's day until the twentieth century. It dominated American foreign policy for so long because it worked in the light of America's enduring geography and the strategic circumstances of the times. America's geography, surrounded by those "big, beautiful oceans," makes it inherently very secure. It could only be threatened by a country strong enough to project major forces across the Atlantic or the Pacific.

In the nineteenth century only the great powers of Europe had even the remotest chance of acquiring such strength. To do that they would first have to dominate all the other European great powers, neutralising them as rivals and absorbing their power and resources. But that couldn't happen as long as the European states preserved the balance of power between them. This they were all determined to do, because they all wanted to avoid being dominated. As long as the European balance of power was preserved without American intervention, no country would be strong enough to threaten America behind its ocean bastions. That meant America had no need to shoulder the immense burdens and risks of intervening strategically in the world beyond its hemisphere. And that worked because, remarkably, the European balance of power did hold from the final defeat of Napoleon in 1815 to the catastrophe of 1914.

Of course America's wide oceans offered no protection from threats *within* the Western Hemisphere, so in 1823 America declared under the Monroe Doctrine that it would oppose any attempt by an outside power to build up a position in the Americas from which it could threaten the United States. The Monroe Doctrine and isolationism thus worked together to keep America secure at very little cost over the century during which it grew from a colonial outpost to become the strongest country in the world.

So why did America abandon it? Isolationism stopped working for America because Europe's balance of power collapsed in the twentieth century, when rising powers upset the old strategic equilibrium. There followed a series of bitter contests – World War I, World War II and the Cold War – in which the strongest of these powers, first Germany and then the Soviet Union, seemed intent on dominating not just Europe but all of Asia – the entire Eurasian supercontinent. For America, this posed a new and potent danger. As one of America's most influential strategists, Zbigniew Brzezinski, wrote, "A power that dominates 'Eurasia' would control two of the world's three most advanced and economically productive regions." Such a power would be strong enough to directly threaten America itself. Therefore, he wrote, "How America 'manages' Eurasia is critical." This new danger was what drove America in the twentieth century to abandon isolationism in favour of global strategic engagement. It was to stop any single power or coalition growing strong enough to threaten America itself by dominating Eurasia. It intervened in World War I, when Russia's collapse gave Germany a real chance of a victory that would have made it master not just of Europe but of Eurasia. It intervened again in late 1941, when the Axis powers seemed poised to dominate Asia, Europe and everything in between.

And it remained engaged after 1945, when the Soviet Union seemed poised to dominate Eurasia. This is what the Cold War was all about. The costs and risks were enormous, but the imperatives were seen to be even bigger because America's very survival seemed to be at stake. That is why it made sense for America to maintain massive military commitments around Eurasia. Isolationism was dead, and the word itself became pejorative. No one wanted to be called an isolationist.

And then the Soviet Union collapsed, and the threat that it might pose to America disappeared. At first, as if by reflex, something of the old isolationism returned. It made a kind of sense to think that with the old adversary gone and no new ones in sight, America could revert to old ways and once again withdraw to its own hemisphere. But that reflex did not prevail. Instead, Americans revived a vision first articulated by Henry Luce in 1941 of a world in harmony and at peace under US leadership. He called it "the American Century." It was, and remains, a very appealing, almost utopian idea – at least when compared with the alternatives. And in the 1990s it seemed within reach.

What a decade that was. With the Soviet Union gone, America suddenly found itself in an unprecedented position of unchallengeable global pre-eminence in every dimension of national power – economic, technological, military, diplomatic and cultural. With communism defeated and, so it seemed, utterly discredited, American ideas and ideals had emerged victorious from the twentieth century's fierce ideological contests. Liberal democracy and market economics now appeared to be the only credible political ideology. A wave of democratisation and market-based economic reform transformed countries around the world. From Washington it looked as if the whole world was being remade in America's image under American leadership.

Not surprisingly, Americans of many stripes eagerly embraced the extraordinary global role that had so suddenly and unexpectedly fallen into their lap. To the idealists it fulfilled an abiding belief, dating back to the *Mayflower*, in America's destiny as a beacon and inspiration to the world.

To hard-headed realists it offered a world in which America's security and prosperity were assured. For almost a century US policymakers had wrestled with the problem of preventing a rival power from dominating Eurasia and the world. Now they could dismiss that problem by dominating Eurasia and the world themselves. And of course it looked like a lot of fun. Policymakers in Washington were understandably intoxicated by the thought that they would, almost literally, rule the world. It seemed to everyone the ultimate vindication of American exceptionalism.

And best of all, it seemed that global leadership was going to be cheap and easy, because America's position would be essentially uncontested. The only countries that resisted the new unipolar order were relatively weak rogue states like Iraq, Iran and North Korea, and it seemed that they could be easily dealt with. This was spectacularly demonstrated in 1991, when Iraq's invasion of Kuwait was effortlessly crushed by America at the head of a vast and diverse global coalition.

Most importantly, it seemed that America would face no great-power rivals. All the world's more powerful states – the Europeans, Russia, China and Japan especially – seemed content to live in a US-led world. With the old ideological contests now resolved and golden economic opportunities open to all in a globalising world, there seemed no danger that America would ever face a major-power rival again. And there seemed no doubt that any rival that did emerge would be swiftly and easily deterred by America's overwhelming military superiority.

This meant that America could lead the post–Cold War world without carrying the exceptional burdens of the previous fifty years. Since 1941 it had made immense sacrifices to prevent the emergence of a Eurasian hegemon. Since the early 1950s that included the extraordinary and quite unprecedented risk of a nuclear war, which could devastate the homeland. Now it could harvest a peace dividend, bring a lot of soldiers home, cease living with the threat of nuclear catastrophe and still lead the world. No wonder they embraced it all so eagerly.

*

Today, thirty-five years after the end of the Cold War, this utopian vision of the world and America's place in it still dominates the thinking of Washington's old – pre-Trumpian – foreign policy establishment. That includes Joe Biden and his team. None of them wants to be called an isolationist.

But the world has changed. It is no longer the world into which America stepped to prevent a rival power dominating the globe, as it did in World War II and the Cold War. Nor is it the world in which, after the Cold War, America became the world's dominant power. Two big things have turned out differently from the way they seemed in the 1990s. First, America's global leadership faces much bigger challenges than Washington expected in the 1990s, when it seemed the US-led order would be essentially uncontested by any major power. That means America faces much higher costs and risks to maintain leadership. Second, the imperative for America to maintain that leadership is not as strong as it was in the twentieth century. The old fear that Eurasia could fall under the control of a single power is now much more remote, because something like the old balance of power has returned.

As a result of these two big changes, the foundational cost–benefit calculus that underpins America's broad strategic posture has switched. A version of isolationism now makes much more sense than the post–Cold War vision of US global primacy. That makes it virtually inevitable that the US-led global order will pass. It has nothing really to do with Donald Trump. It is because in the world as it is, the costs and risks to America of sustaining global leadership outweigh the imperatives to do so. As a policy it no longer adds up.

The primary driver of these changes is the truly fundamental shift in the global distribution of wealth and power over the past four decades, and especially since the turn of the century. This is embodied above all in the economic rise of the two most populous states, China and India. In the 1990s, America had by far the world's biggest economy, the deepest technology sector and an overwhelming preponderance of military power, and it was almost universally believed that this would remain true for decades to come – if not forever. Now China has overtaken America to become the biggest economy in the world on the measure that really matters strategically – purchasing power parity (PPP). The speed of the shift is remarkable. On International Monetary Fund estimates, in 2000 China's economy was one-third the size of America's in PPP terms, and India's was one-fifth. Today China's economy is 30 per cent bigger than America's, and India's is half the size of America's. China has at the same time become a world leader in many key technologies, and has built military forces, especially air and naval forces, that rival America's. India is moving more slowly and taking a different path to wealth and power than China, but it too will probably overtake America's GDP before 2050.

China's rise feels like an old and familiar story, but we in the West still do not understand its full significance. It decisively marks the end of the long era that began 250 years ago, when the Industrial Revolution completely transformed the global distribution of wealth, concentrating it in the countries of northern Europe and North America. Today, for the first time since around 1800, the biggest economy in the world is neither Britain's nor America's, but China's. That changes everything, because wealth is the deepest foundation of national power, and national power is the primary driver of international relations.

In the 1990s, US global leadership looked easy because America seemed so much more powerful than any potential rival. Now in East Asia it confronts a rival that is as strong or stronger than America on many dimensions of national power. This means that confronting and containing China to preserve US global leadership will cost a lot more than Washington insiders imagined in the 1990s, or have been willing to acknowledge since.

And at the same time as the costs of global leadership are going up, the imperatives to defend it are weakening because in today's world America need no longer fear the emergence of a Eurasian hegemon. That danger loomed in the twentieth century because the distribution of wealth and power made it possible that Germany or the Soviet Union could dominate the supercontinent.

That was especially true at the end of World War II and in the early decades of the Cold War, when American fears of a Eurasian hegemon were greatest. The Soviet Union then was by a huge margin the strongest country in Eurasia. Without America's active intervention it could easily have dominated Western Europe and Japan, both still devastated after the war. China after 1949 was a subordinate communist ally, while Southeast Asia and India were vulnerable as well.

That is why America shouldered the immense burden of containing the Soviet Union. But today the distribution of power across Eurasia is very different, thanks especially to the rise of China and India, and also to Europe's clear potential to coalesce as a fourth Eurasian great power. This new distribution of power means that no country, not even China, has the potential to dominate that Moscow once had. The other Eurasian great powers have the weight to balance China and frustrate a Chinese bid to dominate Eurasia.

Some people fear that the new Eurasian balance is threatened by the "no limits" partnership between China and Russia. It is argued that together these two powers could dominate Eurasia, threaten America and replace the US-led liberal-democratic global order with a new authoritarian hegemony that would threaten democracies everywhere. These fears are unfounded. They underestimate what drives Russia. It is determined to assert its own place as a great power, subordinate to no one – including China. That aligns it with China in wanting to replace US global primacy with a multipolar world order. But it will resist Chinese hegemony with all its power. And in doing that it can expect a lot of support – from Europe, India, perhaps also Japan.

The big point here is that in the twenty-first century, thanks to the extraordinary growth of emerging economies, wealth and power is already, and will increasingly be, distributed much more evenly between a number of great powers than it was in the twentieth century. That means America today is relatively weaker than it was, which makes it much harder to preserve the 1990s vision of US global dominance. But it also means America has much less reason than it once did to fear that any *other* country will achieve that kind of dominance, and hence be able to threaten the United States directly. In this crucial sense the twenty-first century is more like the nineteenth century, when the global balance of power worked to prevent global hegemony without active US intervention, than it is like the twentieth century, when America had to intervene in Eurasia against the most powerful states to maintain the balance of power and avoid hegemony. So what has changed is not just that the costs of US global leadership are higher than expected. The imperatives that drove US strategic commitments in Europe and Asia in the twentieth century are far weaker today.

This is the tide that, with or without Trump, is sweeping America away from the old vision of US leadership and back towards some version of isolationism. Indeed, as we will see, this tide drove much of what the Biden administration did, even as they swam against it. But Trump is swimming with this tide, which means his radical transformation of America's role is going to stick.

But that is not all. There is a second big factor overturning the cost–benefit calculus of global leadership for America. It is the return of nuclear weapons to centre-stage in power politics. After the Cold War, nuclear weapons suddenly seemed much less important than they had been in the decades of US–Soviet rivalry. Then the delicate balance of nuclear terror was the primary factor in global strategic affairs and the risk of nuclear war permeated every aspect of great-power politics. But with the demise of the Soviet Union, it appeared that nuclear war was no longer a serious possibility, and that nuclear weapons would play a much less significant part in world affairs. No one seriously feared that America might ever have to fight a nuclear war to defend its post–Cold War global position.

That is not how things have turned out. As America's rivalries with China and Russia have steadily escalated over the past ten or fifteen years, it has become increasingly clear that those rivalries could lead to nuclear war. We will explore later how this works and what it means in both Europe and Asia. The key point is that, as the Ukraine crisis has made abundantly clear, the costs to America of sustaining global leadership against the challenges of Russia and China include the real risk of nuclear attack on the United States. And that makes it even more certain that for America the costs of maintaining that leadership far outweigh the imperative to do so. That, too, explains why we have to take America's abandonment of global leadership so seriously.

*

What happens when America steps back from the role which has defined the global order for over three decades? What new order emerges when US leadership is withdrawn, and what role does America play in it? These are critical questions for everyone, including for Australia. It is no use asking Donald Trump, of course. But the answer is clear nonetheless. Instead of a unipolar order dominated by one overwhelmingly powerful leading country, we will see a global multipolar order in which a number of "great powers" play more or less equal roles in shaping world affairs through a complex combination of competition, accommodation and cooperation.

This vision of global order feels very different from the unipolar model of the post–Cold War era, or from the bipolar order of the Cold War, but it is not unfamiliar. A multipolar order was recognised in the creation of the United Nations after World War II, with the collective leadership of five "world powers" embodied in the structure of the Security Council with its five permanent members. It was the shape of the European order from the mid-seventeenth century to the mid-twentieth century. Like those exemplars, the new multipolar order will encompass a wide diversity of political systems and ideologies among the great powers at its core. Much will depend on how they get along – how that complex combination of competition, accommodation and cooperation works in practice. It will always be difficult and sometimes dangerous, but it can be made to work. The example of Europe in the nineteenth century shows how great-power rivalries can be managed to avoid any one power dominating, to allow trade to flourish and (mostly) to keep the peace.

How will America under Trump see this kind of order? Interestingly, Trump's secretary of state, Marco Rubio, who seems by far the most thoughtful of the new administration's senior figures, has spoken about this quite explicitly. In his opening statement to his Senate confirmation hearings, Rubio brusquely dismissed the vision of a US-led liberal world order:

> Out of the triumphalism of the end of long Cold War emerged a bipartisan consensus that we had reached "the end of history." That all the nations of Earth would become members of the democratic Western-led community. That a foreign policy that served the national interest could now be replaced by one that served the "liberal world order." And that all mankind was now destined to abandon national identity, and we would become "one human family" and "citizens of the world." This wasn't just a fantasy; it was a dangerous delusion.

A few weeks later he explained that a multipolar order was taking its place.

> It's not normal for the world to simply have a unipolar power. That was not – that was an anomaly. It was a product of the end of the Cold War, but eventually you were going to reach back to a point where you had a multipolar world, multi great powers in different parts of the planet. We face that now with China and to some extent Russia …

Of course Trump, not being an ideas person, has never spoken in these terms. Indeed, it may appear unlikely that a man so obsessed with American greatness would agree with Rubio that America should step back from global leadership to take its place as an equal partner with other great powers in a multipolar global order. But in fact this vision meshes perfectly with Trump's trademark instincts and prejudices, and with his own distinctive way of defining America's greatness. It fits with his respect for other strong countries and their leaders, including Xi Jinping and Vladimir Putin. It fits with his acceptance that they want to exert influence over their neighbours just as he asserts America's sphere of influence in the Western Hemisphere. It fits, too, with his lifelong rejection of America's alliances in Europe and Asia, which are a vital foundation of US global leadership.

And it suits Trump's taste for ruthless dealing. For generations American leaders have tried to avoid the morally ambiguous compromises and accommodations of multipolar great-power politics, which they have seen as incompatible with the moral clarity of American exceptionalism. In different ways isolationism and unipolar leadership both offered refuge from such distasteful necessities. Trump has no such qualms. He likes the idea of cutting deals with powerful rivals in the ceaseless pursuit of advantage, and doesn't mind that smaller, weaker players get done over in the process. That is his idea of fun.

Nonetheless, it remains unclear how he sees America participating in the new multipolar order. On the one hand, we can expect him to claim a place as "first among equals" at the top table of great powers. On the other hand, he will reject any suggestion that America should accept responsibilities or shoulder burdens to support global order that do not directly serve narrow US interests. He will be an awkward partner in making the multipolar world work. His instinct for bullying, his disdain for institutions, his gleeful delight in breaking rules and issuing demands – all these will make it hard for America to play a constructive role in creating the norms and habits which will underpin the new order. And his policies and instincts will take America out of the running on many urgent issues – such as climate change, disaster relief and pandemic prevention – that require collective global solutions. By abolishing America's international aid agency, USAID, for example, Trump has apparently destroyed America's capacity to help save lives in natural disaster emergencies.

Where Trump does intervene in global issues, his contribution is unlikely to be helpful. As we will see, his instinct that there is no alternative to a compromise peace between Russia and Ukraine is correct, but his approach to brokering that peace has been gravely flawed. Trump's plan for Gaza is an absurd abomination but makes it harder for more just and workable proposals to appear. And his renewed approach to dealing with Iran's nuclear weapons program looks no more likely to work than his strange courtship of North Korea did eight years ago. It will be interesting to see how Trump balances Netanyahu's eagerness for military strikes on Iran's nuclear facilities with his own reluctance to be drawn into military entanglements. My hunch is that he will continue to be cautious.

The Middle East nonetheless remains something of an exception to Trump's instinct to let the rest of the world look after its own problems. That is partly because of the region's, and especially Israel's, tenacious grip on the American conservative mind, and partly because it seems to offer the prospect of profit. This will do nothing to help manage the region's problems. But, then, neither did his predecessors' approach. The Biden administration talked up their commitment to a US-led order based on international law but did nothing effective to constrain a close ally from committing what are, quite clearly, very serious war crimes.

It should not have been hard for the Biden administration to work out a response to the tragedy in Gaza that matched its professed commitment to avowed values and international law. The argument is not, after all, so very complex. Israel has a right to exist within secure and internationally recognised borders. The Palestinians have the right to a state in the West Bank and Gaza. Israel has refused to countenance the establishment of such a state. That does not justify Hamas's crimes on and since 7 October 2023. Equally, those crimes do not justify Israel's assault on Gaza since then. Both sides are deeply in the wrong.

Upon that basis the Biden administration could have constructed a policy that accorded with its claims to global leadership. Instead, seemingly from sheer moral and political weakness, it went along with the Netanyahu government's crimes, tacitly adopting the view so neatly described by Tom Stevenson: "Any violence committed by Palestinians justifies all violence by Israel, and no violence committed by Israel justifies any by Palestinians." That is the opposite of leadership. Trump's policies on Gaza are, of course, even worse, but they are less hypocritical. He doesn't pretend to defend universal values, international law and the old vision of US global leadership. In this respect the most prodigious liar in the history of US politics is more honest than his opponents.

There will be more hard choices to come. Embracing a multipolar world order means accepting authoritarian regimes like Russia and China as peers and equal participants in international politics. To some, that means compromising principles and values which US global leadership was supposed to foster and defend. But as we will see, the alternative carries very real risks of major war. There is no escaping the need to decide how these conflicting policy and moral imperatives should be balanced. This is one of the great questions of our time. In today's world the threat to peace comes as much, or indeed more, from efforts to preserve the US-led unipolar order as from efforts to replace it with a multipolar order. In this respect, at least, Trump's willingness to see America take its place in a multipolar order is something to be grateful for.

America's allies around the world might one day be grateful, too, for the way Trump has smashed their illusions about the new realities of global power which they have been ignoring for so long. From Europe to Asia, in the face of all the evidence, they have convinced themselves that America will always retain the strength and resolve to guarantee their security. Now, thanks to Trump, they are brought face to face with the need for long-overdue policy revolutions of their own. Nowhere is this more brutally true than in Europe, as the Europeans face the test of Ukraine.

The war in Ukraine is a tragedy for the people of Ukraine and, one might add, for the people of Russia. But much more has been at stake there than the future of Ukraine, or the security of other countries on Russia's borders. The Russian invasion has become a decisive test of the US-led global order that has supposedly seen America take primary responsibility for the security of major regions around the world, including Europe and East Asia. It may indeed turn out to be *the* decisive test of that order, and it is now clear that the test has been failed. We still do not know when and on what terms the present fighting will end. But it is clear that after more than three years of war, at terrible cost, Ukraine faces the loss of a lot of land and people, limits on its relations with the rest of Europe, and continued vulnerability to future Russian aggression.

It is easy to blame Donald Trump for this. He certainly deserves a lot of blame for the way he has leaned towards Moscow and bullied Kyiv, making its difficult situation a lot worse. But Trump is not the cause of Ukraine's predicament, which was clear and inescapable long before Trump won his second term. It has been Ukraine's fate to be the place where Washington's illusions about America's place in the world have collided most directly with the strategic realities of our age.

The Russo–Ukrainian War marks the end of America's strategic leadership in Europe, and signals very plainly the transition from the US-led global order of the post–Cold War era to the new multipolar order.

The war is so significant in this transition because of what it shows about the relative power and resolve of the rival powers involved. Any international order is defined ultimately by the issues on which the strongest powers – the great powers – can convince one another they are willing to go to war with one another over. That is because an international order defines the diplomatic frame within which countries interact, and the boundaries of that frame are set by the points at which diplomacy gives way to war.

We can see how this worked in the past. The nineteenth-century multipolar Concert of Europe was defined by the clear willingness of all the European great powers to go to war to prevent any one of them becoming strong enough to dominate the rest. The bipolar Cold War order was defined by the clear willingness of both superpowers to go to war to prevent the other from upsetting the status quo by intruding into the other's spheres of influence. The unipolar post–Cold War order has been defined ultimately by America's presumed willingness to go to war to prevent any rival from contesting the US claim to be the world's sole great power and establishing a sphere of influence from which it sought to exclude America.

This presumption has been tested in Ukraine and found to be false. That is what Moscow hoped and intended. Russia's aim in Ukraine has been not just to acquire territory but to re-establish itself as the great power in its own region, and a co-equal with America and other major powers in the global multipolar order. America and its allies have not been willing to go to war to stop it, and by failing to defend the unipolar order they have acquiesced in its replacement by a multipolar order.

The Russo–Ukrainian War has proved to be very significant in another way, too. It has shown the decisive role that nuclear weapons play in contemporary power politics. On most measures, Russia hardly ranks as a great power in comparison with America, China, Europe or even India. Russia's success in facing down America in Ukraine – and yes, that is what it has done – cannot be explained by the size of its GDP, the quality of its technology or the strength of its conventional (non-nuclear) armed forces. Moscow has been able to deter America and US allies from an effective response to its invasion of Ukraine primarily because of the threat posed by its nuclear arsenal. We should not be surprised to learn once again how decisive nuclear threats can be in a great-power confrontation.

*

In America and among its Western allies, including here in Australia, the months after Russia's invasion of Ukraine were a time of anger and anxiety, of course, but also a time of growing clarity and confidence. After years of mounting concern about Chinese and Russian strategic ambitions, the outbreak of the first full-scale war in Europe since 1945 made things seem suddenly clear. Everyone agreed that much more was at stake than the fate of Ukraine. As a point of principle, Russia was violating the central dictum of the UN Charter, that aggression by one country against another could never be accepted. But more important, as a point of practical power politics, Russia was defying the foundational precept of the post–Cold War order: that no country other than America could be a great power and try to exclude America from its close neighbourhood.

Governments and commentators further argued that Russia's actions showed the scale of the threat to global order more broadly. It confirmed fears that the two leading authoritarian powers, which had declared a "no-limits" partnership just days before the invasion, were apparently willing to go to any lengths to overturn the US-led global order. If Ukraine wasn't saved, surely Taiwan would be next. The Russian invasion therefore threatened US allies everywhere, because we all depended on the US-led order for our security.

That made it clear how the West must respond. If Russia was willing to go to war to overturn the international order, then America and its allies had to be willing to pull together and do whatever was necessary to defeat Russia and defend the order – not just from Russia, but from China too.

It therefore seemed obvious that Russia's invasion must be defeated so decisively that it would abandon its great-power ambitions. Any kind of negotiated outcome that rewarded Moscow's aggression would be a disaster comparable to Neville Chamberlain's blunder at Munich in 1938.

But while all this was very worrying, those first few months of the Russo–Ukrainian War were also rather encouraging. A steady flow of good news made it seem that defeating Russia and defending the US-led order was not going to be all that hard. Ukraine surprised the world with brilliant early successes on the battlefield, culminating in the spectacular counteroffensives of late 2022, which won back much of the territory that Russia had seized in February and March. Meanwhile the countries of the West rushed to help Ukraine with unexpected speed and zeal. They imposed massive economic sanctions on Moscow and launched huge programs of military and economic aid for Kyiv.

This seemed to be the Biden administration's finest hour. Just six months after the humiliatingly chaotic withdrawal from Afghanistan, they looked strong and decisive in leading a united Western response. The Europeans rallied behind Ukraine and began to talk, at least, of taking defence seriously again. Sweden and Finland abandoned their long-cherished neutrality and joined NATO. US allies in Asia were drawn in to face the common challenge. For a time, it seemed that everything was going Ukraine's, and the West's, way. By the end of 2022 the invasion looked like a mortifying military disaster for Moscow, and its much-vaunted army appeared close to collapse. So did its economy, battered by some of the toughest sanctions the world had ever seen. Moscow seemed headed for exactly the humiliating defeat that everyone in the West called for.

Best of all, it seemed that this essential outcome could be achieved at relatively little cost and very little strategic risk to America and its allies. They would send weapons and money, but Ukraine would do all the fighting. It was a cheering prospect as long as a decisive Ukrainian victory seemed within reach.

But that illusion began to fade in mid-2023. The West expected that a Ukrainian summer offensive would inflict further decisive defeats on Russia like those it suffered in late 2022. Instead, the offensive faltered and died on well-prepared Russian defences.

There were several reasons for this disappointment. The Russian army learnt from its mistakes and performed better than expected. Western economic sanctions were less effective in choking Moscow's military effort than predicted, in part because China and India helped the Russians evade them. New technologies, especially drones, upset established military doctrines. In particular, their ability to provide almost continuous surveillance of areas behind the battlefront made it virtually impossible to concentrate large forces undetected for an offensive assault. That gave defence a big advantage over offence, which made it easier for Russia to hold Ukrainian territory and harder for Ukraine to expel it. Kyiv had some home-grown problems too, especially in recruiting enough soldiers to defend a long front line.

By the end of that summer, it was clear that neither side had any real hope of decisive battlefield victories. Instead, they faced a long war of attrition, in which Russia had important advantages. Its army, though humiliated by the debacles of 2022, had not been broken. Its people had not deserted their leaders and its economy had not collapsed, and ultimately its bigger population was better able to absorb and sustain the horrendous casualties suffered on both sides. The situation should have been clear. Even with a lot of Western financial support and weapons, Ukraine fighting alone could not decisively defeat Russia. The only way to stop the fighting was to negotiate a compromise, which would, inevitably, mean yielding to some of Russia's demands.

Nonetheless, the conviction that Ukraine should and would fight on until Russia was decisively defeated lingered for a long time. In Kyiv, President Zelenskyy clung to the courageous and defiant rhetoric which had for so long inspired both Ukrainians and their Western supporters. Leaders and commentators in the West likewise found it hard to step back from the Churchillian postures they had so boldly adopted in 2022.

It is easy to see why the idea of a compromise peace was so repugnant. Surrendering Ukrainian territory to Russia would leave Ukrainian citizens at Moscow's mercy, and of course there could be no guarantee that it would end there. A deal to end the fighting would allow Russia to recover, rebuild and return to the attack. Conceding any of Moscow's diplomatic demands, such as keeping Ukraine out of NATO, would leave Ukraine forever under Russia's thumb. It would also threaten the rest of Europe, because if Russia was not stopped in Ukraine, where would it be stopped? Above all, it would seriously weaken the US-led order around the world – including in Asia.

The government in Kyiv and many commentators in the West argued that Ukraine could still defeat Russia if it got more weapons from the West, with fewer restrictions on using them to strike deep into Russia. But the

Ukrainians gradually received much of what they wanted, including tanks, combat aircraft, longer-range missiles and the nod for deep strikes, but they didn't deliver a war-winning edge. That was because on the conventional battlefield Russia had a structural advantage.

To succeed, Russian forces need only to hold the Ukrainian territory they have occupied, while Ukraine has to dislodge them – a much harder task. So by the end of 2023 it was plain that Ukraine could not defeat Russia on the battlefield by itself. And over 2024 it became increasing clear that by a narrow but critical margin the battlefield advantage actually lay with Russia. But there was a deeper problem. No matter how well the Ukrainians fought, and no matter how much support they got from the West – even if NATO members had sent combat forces to the front line, which they seem never to have even contemplated – there remained an insuperable barrier to Ukrainian victory: Russia's nuclear weapons.

*

Russia's invasion of Ukraine has brought nuclear weapons and the threat of nuclear war back to the central position in international politics that they occupied throughout the Cold War. When the Cold War ended, people around the world felt enormous relief that the intense, but now largely forgotten, fear of a nuclear holocaust had apparently disappeared. Their relief was only partly justified by the sharp cuts to the superpowers' nuclear forces from the almost unimaginable levels of the Cold War – 60,000 warheads between them in the mid-1980s. Each still retains around 6000 nuclear warheads, and that is more than enough to produce the truly unimaginable global catastrophe that we feared until 1989 and so quickly forgot afterwards.

It takes an effort of the imagination to grasp that, right now, sufficient nuclear weapons to create that catastrophe are poised ready to be used at a few hours' or even a few minutes' notice. The intercontinental ballistic missiles stand in their silos, the launch crews at their consoles and the launch codes in the safes nearby. The ballistic missile submarines are at sea, their missiles and warheads ready to go. All the machinery of a full-scale nuclear war is poised for immediate action. All that is missing is the decision to go. And yet for over three decades, Washington and its Western allies have largely ignored the significance of this extraordinary situation as a factor in international affairs.

This made a kind of sense when it seemed that the other major powers that possess nuclear weapons – China and Russia, especially – accepted America as the world's leading power. While that remained true, they could have no disagreements with America that would possibly justify using them. But it made less and less sense as America's nuclear-armed rivals increasingly challenged its claims to primacy. One reason for the complacency is that China, as the more formidable rival, still had relatively few nuclear weapons, so US strategists found it hard to take China seriously as a nuclear adversary. Another reason is that, even as China's and Russia's challenge grew, Washington remained convinced that neither rival was serious enough to contemplate pushing things so far as nuclear war. Vladimir Putin has now dispelled that illusion. So, in a different way, has Beijing, as we will see later.

But perhaps the most important reason why America and its allies have for so long downplayed the significance of nuclear weapons is that they raise a very awkward question. Is Washington willing to fight a nuclear war to defend the post–Cold War order, as it had been willing to do to contain the Soviets in the Cold War? This is a question that no one in Washington wanted to consider too carefully, because they suspected the answer would be "no." Now Putin has forced them to confront it, and Joe Biden gave the answer they all feared. Even before the invasion, he promised that, whatever happened, America would not go to war to defend Ukraine because, as he repeatedly said, "We will not fight the third world war in Ukraine." His meaning was very clear, especially to people like him of the Cold War generation to whom "the third world war" means only one thing – a full-scale nuclear conflict. Biden refused to consider sending troops to Ukraine because he feared that any US combat involvement could lead to a nuclear war and he was not willing to contemplate that.

Was he right to fear this? Was the risk of nuclear war serious enough to deter Washington and its allies from giving Ukraine the only kind of help that would help it to win?

From the start Russia repeatedly issued nuclear threats to play on Washington's fears. Most of the time these threats were aimed at deterring Washington from giving Ukraine more sophisticated weapons or allowing Kyiv to strike targets inside Russia. These threats did not ultimately succeed, because Washington eventually gave Ukraine most of what it asked for. The Biden administration apparently decided these issues were not serious enough to push Moscow across the nuclear threshold, because they correctly judged that such measures would not decisively affect the outcome of the war.

But these were not the nuclear threats that really mattered. In September 2022 Kyiv's spectacular autumn offensives bundled the Russian army out of key positions at Kharkiv and Kherson on the northern and southern ends of the front. Ukraine seemed poised to drive Russia right out of Ukraine, including even from Crimea. At this point fears in Washington spiked, with real concerns that Moscow was seriously considering using nuclear weapons to stop it.

According to Bob Woodward's apparently well-sourced account, US intelligence analysts assessed there was a 50 per cent chance that Putin would authorise the use of tactical nuclear weapons to prevent further losses. Putin certainly spoke as if that was so. "If the territorial integrity of our country is threatened," Putin declared on 21 September 2022, "we will without doubt use all available means to protect Russia and our people – this is not bluff." It might have been tempting to assume that he was in fact bluffing. No country had used a nuclear weapon since Nagasaki in 1945, and to many people it seemed simply unthinkable that Putin would break the "nuclear taboo" that had stood for almost eight decades. But the Biden administration took his threats very seriously, specifically identifying the retaking of Crimea by Ukraine as a "red line" for Putin.

They were right to do so. A decision to use nuclear weapons would have been unprecedented, but so were the circumstances. Since they became nuclear powers, neither Russia nor the Soviet Union before it, nor the United States for that matter, has ever faced a strategic crisis comparable to the one that Putin would have faced had Ukraine's autumn offensives gone much further. After the mortifying reverses suffered in the first weeks of the war, when Ukraine routed his thrust against Kyiv, Putin now confronted the prospect that he would suffer complete and humiliating defeat – exactly the kind of defeat that Washington and its allies were seeking. That would not just have jeopardised his own position of supreme power in Russia. It would have been a fatal blow to his ambition to reclaim Russia's place as a great power, repeating the humiliation of the Soviet collapse in 1991, which Putin himself had described as the greatest strategic disaster of the twentieth century. Facing such a calamity, it would be surprising if Putin had not seriously considered the nuclear option.

Fortunately it did not come to that, for which the Biden administration claimed some credit. They asked China to intervene by warning Russia "not to go there," and later claimed that Beijing's intervention helped convince Moscow not to use nuclear weapons. That seems unlikely. If Russia faced a disastrous defeat, it is hard to see how mere diplomatic pressure, even from Beijing, would have carried much weight. With so much at stake, the only real constraint would have been a credible threat of military retaliation. Washington tried that too. The Biden administration publicly and privately warned Moscow that America would inflict unspecified "catastrophic" consequences if Russia used nuclear weapons. But it is not clear those threats had any effect either, because the battlefield crisis passed; by late October, Ukraine's counteroffensives had run out of steam. Russia's conventional forces stabilised the front, so Moscow didn't need to contemplate nuclear attacks to avoid complete defeat.

But what happened that northern autumn raises vital questions for Ukraine and Europe, with huge implications for the entire international order. What would have happened if, then or later, Ukraine had come within sight of the decisive victory that Kyiv and its Western supporters sought? What would have deterred Putin from using nuclear weapons against Ukraine, if that was the only way to prevent a complete Russian defeat? What kind of "catastrophic" retaliation could Washington credibly threaten that would have looked worse to Putin than that?

The Biden team never spelt out publicly what kind of retaliation they were threatening in those tense weeks in 2022. They could not have imagined that further diplomatic or economic sanctions would be enough, so it seemed that Biden would have to threaten to break his promise and send America itself to war with Russia. But it is very unlikely that Biden threatened to use nuclear weapons at that time. Instead, the talk in Washington was of US military strikes with conventional weapons against Russian military and military-industrial targets. But how credible would that threat have been? Realistically, the only option America had to impose "catastrophic" consequences on Russia – and to work they would have to have seemed to the Kremlin *more* catastrophic than total defeat in Ukraine – would have been to use nuclear weapons. And that would have run a very serious risk of a Russian nuclear counterattack on the United States itself. In the light of that risk, would Putin have taken Washington's threats seriously? Would he really have believed that Biden would risk New York and Washington to save Ukraine? Or would he have called Biden's bluff?

As they stood together on the brink of nuclear war, each side would have to weigh the other side's threats and the resolve that lay behind them, to determine which of them was more likely to be bluffing. But Russia would have a clear advantage in that perilous psychological contest, because both sides would know that the stakes in Ukraine are higher for Russia than for America. That means both sides know that Moscow is less likely to be bluffing than Washington, which puts Washington at a huge disadvantage in convincing Moscow to back off. Washington could not afford to dismiss Russia's threats as a bluff. As Biden's secretary of state, Antony Blinken, said in January 2025, looking back on this moment, "When it comes to nuclear weapons, nothing is more serious." So Washington would almost certainly have backed down. Indeed, Biden had already done so when he declared that America would not fight "the third world war" over Ukraine. Moscow, recognising this, would not have been deterred from launching nuclear weapons against Ukraine, to which Ukraine had no response.

In fact, Russia would not even need to launch a nuclear weapon. The threat alone would very likely be enough to make Ukraine back off. What could Ukraine have done if in October 2022 Russia had declared that it would use tactical nuclear weapons unless Ukraine ceased its counteroffensive and withdrew? This is called nuclear blackmail, and it works. America used it against China several times over Taiwan in the 1950s, before China got nuclear weapons. Lacking a credible counterthreat, Kyiv would have had no choice but to comply, as the Chinese did in the 1950s, and Moscow would have prevailed without firing a nuclear shot.

The reality is that when truly vital interests are at stake, as they are for Russia in Ukraine, the only way to deter the use of nuclear weapons is with an equally credible threat of nuclear retaliation from the other side, with all the dangers that entails. There are no credible deterrent options that avoid the risk of nuclear war.

In a sense this is not a new predicament for Washington. During the Cold War there were always doubts on both sides of the Atlantic about whether Washington was really willing to risk nuclear attacks on America itself by using its nuclear forces to defeat a Soviet assault on Western Europe. US strategists looked for ways to get round this by planning for a "limited" nuclear war in which both sides refrained from attacks on one another's homelands. That looked like an appealing way to defend US interests in Europe while minimising the nuclear risks to America.

The problem was that it proved impossible to be even remotely confident that a limited nuclear war would not swiftly escalate to a full-scale nuclear holocaust. In the 1980s Australia's own scholar Des Ball made a major contribution to debunking the "limited war" illusion, and the arguments he developed still hold good today. So in the end America's Cold War deterrent relied on convincing the Soviets that America really was ultimately willing to risk nuclear attack on US cities to defend Western Europe, which it successfully did. Likewise, today Washington could only deter nuclear attacks on Ukraine if it could convince Moscow that it was willing to risk nuclear attacks on America itself. And no one believed that it was.

This has profound and disturbing implications for the whole Ukraine conflict. It means that Ukraine, facing a nuclear-armed Russia and with no nuclear deterrent of its own, could never have achieved the victory it sought over Russia. If at any point Ukraine seemed poised for such a victory, Russia could have credibly threatened to use nuclear weapons to stop it, because Ukraine's supporters had no credible way to deter Moscow from carrying out those threats.

Why cannot America deter Russia today in the way it deterred the Soviets in the Cold War? The difference is in the balance of resolve. In the Cold War both sides were equally determined to preserve the status quo between them and prevent any significant shift in the bipolar global order in the other side's favour. In the critical theatres of Europe and Northeast Asia, both Moscow and Washington were convinced that even a small win for the other side might have catastrophic consequences. It could undermine the credibility of their entire position, leading to a collapse which left their rival victorious and posing an existential threat to their country and way of life. That is why both sides were willing to spend enormous sums on weapons to defend their respective positions, and were willing to run the almost unimaginable risk of a nuclear war rather than suffer even small defeats in the critical theatres.

Today we might doubt the wisdom of those judgements, and many doubted them at the time. But we can hardly doubt that this was the consistent position of both superpowers. Each was equally and utterly committed to preserving the status quo between them, and each understood and accepted that the other's resolve was as strong as its own. This is what kept the bipolar order between them so stable for so long, and prevented war from breaking out.

What was called at the time "the delicate balance of terror" in fact rested on a clearly understood balance of resolve. It was essential that each side believed the other side's resolve was just as strong as its own, and that had to be demonstrated convincingly. Washington made its resolve clear to

Moscow both by what it did and by what it said. It created and maintained an unprecedented network of peacetime alliances which committed America to the defence of nations far from its shores. It built massive conventional armed forces and maintained many of them permanently in Europe and Asia. It fought costly wars in Korea and Vietnam when it believed, rightly or wrongly, that the status quo with the Soviets was in danger. And of course it built immense new nuclear forces. Underlying all of this, it spent massive amounts on defence – as much as 15 per cent of GDP in the early 1950s and still 6 to 7 per cent in the 1980s. All this helped to convince the Soviets that America was willing to fight a nuclear war to defend its allies in Europe and Northeast Asia, even though they lay thousands of kilometres from America across wide oceans.

But perhaps equally important was what US leaders said. During the Cold War they spoke very frankly to the American people about the risks they had to face to contain the Soviet Union. At critical moments they explicitly declared that if necessary America would use nuclear weapons, and they acknowledged that America could suffer nuclear attack in return.

The most famous instance is the Cuban Missile Crisis of 1962, but an even more telling example is the Berlin Crisis the previous year, when President Kennedy faced Soviet demands for the withdrawal of US and allied forces from West Berlin. At the height of the crisis, Kennedy delivered a televised national address in which he committed America to defend its position in West Berlin, acknowledged that this could lead to nuclear war, and instructed America to prepare to face a nuclear attack. The Kremlin backed down, US forces stayed in West Berlin, and the Berlin Wall went up instead. Kennedy's explicit threat is a perfect example of a vital principle that is as true today as it was in the Cold War: that a nuclear power can be stopped, but only by an unambiguous demonstration of willingness to fight a nuclear war to stop it.

This is precisely what successive US administrations in recent years have failed to do as the challenges to US primacy have grown. It is not as if they haven't seen the challenges coming, because they have been unmistakably clear for a long time. In Europe it is almost twenty years since Vladimir Putin told the world very bluntly that Russia did not accept the US-led order. It is seventeen years since he invaded Georgia, showing that he would use force to restore Russia's claim to a sphere of influence over its neighbours. It is eleven years since Russia seized Crimea and occupied other parts of Ukraine.

In response there have been countless broad declarations of America's desire to defend and preserve its global leadership. But over this time there have been no material changes to America's military capacity remotely comparable to the massive measures it took to confront and contain the Soviet challenge in the decades after 1945. Its military posture today in Europe has not increased significantly from the levels reached at the end of the post–Cold War run-down in the 1990s. US defence spending as a share of GDP is now at the same level as it was in 1999, before the War on Terror. That was the level that seemed right when America believed it would face no great-power rivals. It looks absurd today.

Equally important is that, unlike their Cold War predecessors, US leaders over the past twenty years have failed to prepare the American people for the costs and risks they would have to bear to defend US global leadership from the powerful challengers of today. Nor have they explained why Americans should bear those costs and risks. They have said that US global leadership must be defended, but have not made the case as to why that matters so much to Americans. And that is because, as we have seen, the case is not there to be made. America's strategic stake in Europe is not now what it was in the Cold War, because today it has no reason to fear that a shift in the European balance could open the door to a Eurasian hegemon. The old Washington establishment might argue that America's role as the bulwark of European security is vital to its claim to global leadership, but the truth is that global leadership is not vital to America's own security when the alternative is not a hostile authoritarian hegemony but a diverse and a well-balanced global multipolarity. That is why, ultimately, America cannot defend Ukraine from Russia. That is the reality that Donald Trump, in his weird way, understands.

INTERLUDE: UKRAINE'S PREDICAMENT AND THE FUTURE OF EUROPE

This is all a terrible shock for the Europeans. Since the end of the Cold War, and in the face of mounting evidence over two decades, European leaders and policymakers have held fast to two agreeable assumptions. One was that Russia, though restless and dissatisfied with its place in the post–Cold War world, would not risk a direct military challenge to the security of Europe and America's place as its guardian. The other was that if the first assumption proved to be false and Russia really did threaten Europe, Washington would respond decisively and defeat Russia's challenge. Washington fostered these illusions for decades. For example, it joined other Europeans in eagerly extending strategic commitments under NATO to new countries throughout Eastern Europe, sending a misleading message that it was willing to go to war with Russia to defend them.

Few in America or Europe paused to ask whether the security of the Baltic States, for example, was really so vital to the security of America, or of other European NATO members, to justify risking nuclear war with Russia to defend them. Like Britain's promises to defend France in the 1920s, these commitments "rested on the assumption that the promises given would never have to be made good."

Now the Europeans' illusions are shattered, and not just by Donald Trump. Long before he returned to the White House, it was clear both that the Russians posed the most serious threat to Europe since the Cold War, and that America would not stop them. That leaves the Europeans facing two very scary realities. The first is that Europe will now have to defend itself, regardless of NATO.

It would be foolish to imagine that America would be any more willing to risk nuclear war with Russia to defend a member of NATO than it has been to defend Ukraine. What would matter to America if it faced that momentous choice is not whether a country was a NATO ally or not but whether its defence was vital to America's security. In post–Cold War Europe, and after

NATO's thoughtless expansion, being a member of the alliance no longer guarantees that a country is vital to America's security.

On the contrary, it is not clear today that any country in Europe is vital to America's security, because Washington need no longer fear that by subjugating a defenceless Europe Russia might come to dominate Eurasia and threaten America itself. That is not just because Russia's power in Eurasia would still be balanced by China and India. Even more to the point, Europe can defend itself from Russia. The EU's combined GDP is as much as ten times Russia's, and European NATO members have three times as many tanks and infantry fighting vehicles as Russia, and twice as many fighter aircraft. Europe today has the strategic weight to contain Russia without undue strain, so it makes no strategic sense for America to do it for them.

That has been true for decades, but until Trump, no one said it out loud. His return, coming on top of the failure in Ukraine, has made things clear. But old and comfortable habits are hard to break, and even now some Europeans still hope that America will be there for them. They imagine that meeting Trump's demands for higher defence spending will buy American protection. That is absurd. How much the Europeans spend on defence makes no difference to how important they are to America's security.

The Europeans may find that defending themselves will not be as hard as they fear. They will need to spend more, of course, but probably no more than 3 per cent of their combined GDP if they act cooperatively and spend wisely. But money is not the real problem. It will be harder to replace US leadership with the Europe-wide political and military structures needed to act as a unified strategic power. They have decades of intense continent-wide cooperation under the EU and NATO to build on, but they will need a leader. That can only be Germany, as the strongest country in Europe and because of its position at the strategic centre of the continent. Much will therefore depend on Germany stepping up to this role.

The hardest problem for the Europeans will be creating their own effective nuclear deterrent, which is essential for them to contend with Russia. France and Britain already have nuclear forces which, though far smaller than Russia's, are big enough to offer a robust deterrent. But as long as they remain under French and British control, there will be serious doubts about how credible a counter they are to nuclear threats to countries closer to Russia. Would the Kremlin believe that leaders in Paris and London would be willing to risk nuclear war to defend Poland or Romania?

These questions are already on the table in Europe, but the answers are far from clear. President Macron of France has recently spoken of his willingness for France's nuclear force to provide a deterrent for Europe, but insists that it must remain under sole French control. And he has highlighted the problem with this. *The Economist* has reported that

> In 2022 Mr Macron said he would "evidently" not respond in kind if Russia used nuclear weapons in Ukraine. French vital interests were "clearly defined," he claimed, confusingly, and "these would not be at stake if there was a nuclear ballistic attack in Ukraine" – or, he added, unwisely, "in the region."

That last qualification, whether unwise or not, was hardly surprising. That is why Chancellor Friedrich Merz of Germany has said that he wants to discuss the question with France and Britain and has envisaged "nuclear sharing" arrangements with them. It is hard to see how such arrangements could solve the problem without passing full control of the weapons into pan-European hands, which seems unlikely. It is hard to envisage such a pan-European authority without much closer political integration than anyone has seriously considered until now. That looks especially difficult in today's fractious Europe, where Eurosceptics abound.

Perhaps that is why Merz has said that even with a "European" deterrent, Europe would still have to rely on America's nuclear forces. But that is just wishful thinking. The only real alternative to a credible European nuclear deterrent is for European countries to build their own nuclear weapons. Poland's Prime Minister Donald Tusk has said openly that his country might have to consider that. Many others in Europe are no doubt thinking the same.

How these questions are eventually resolved will be central to the way Europe's new strategic identity develops. But before they get there, the Europeans will have to answer a more pressing question: are they willing to defend Ukraine, or what's left of it, from Russia? And if not, where are they going to draw the line on Russia's ambitions?

This is not a new question. Ever since the late seventeenth century, when Peter the Great turned Russia into a great power and made it a force in European power politics, one of the great and abiding questions for the rest of Europe has been how far west and south they allow Russia's power and influence to spread.

There have been a lot of different answers to that question. In 1814 the Russians got as far west as Paris, having chased Napoleon all the way from Moscow. After World War II they got to Berlin and beyond, and stayed there for decades until the Cold War ended. The subsequent collapse of the Soviet Union in 1991 saw Russia pushed back to its narrowest limits since the Middle Ages, and it ceased for a time to be a great power in Europe. But for most of the past 300 years the Europeans have allowed Russian power to extend about halfway across Poland.

Now the Europeans face this old question again. The invasion of Ukraine is all about reasserting Russia's place as a great power and rebuilding a sphere of influence in Eastern Europe. There is no reason to think that Moscow's ambition will be satisfied with whatever it wins in the settlement of the current Russo–Ukrainian War. The Europeans must prudently recognise the risk that eventually Russia will try to extend its influence further west until it is stopped. It is now up to the Europeans to decide where that will be.

The war in Ukraine has showed that stopping Russia means confronting it directly with superior armed force. It has also taught that to neutralise Russian nuclear blackmail, conventional forces must be backed by a credible threat of nuclear retaliation for any Russian use of nuclear weapons. This helps to define what it means to draw a limit to Russia's ambitions. In the long run Europe will end up conceding to Russia whatever it cannot convince the Kremlin it is willing to fight a nuclear war to deny it. Where might the Europeans set that limit? Of course views across Europe will differ. Poland and the Baltic States will naturally be inclined to set it further east than France or Britain. That helps to explain why Germany's role is so crucial, as the furthest east of the major NATO powers.

There seems no chance now that the Europeans will try to push Russia back to the internationally recognised border with Ukraine. They could, however, decide to stand firm on whatever line emerges from the present peace process as the limit of Russian control. The suggestion that European powers (joined by Australia) might deploy "peacekeeping" forces to monitor and enforce the settlement gestures in this direction. But even if Russia accepted that as part of a settlement, such forces would not constrain Moscow unless they are there to fight (should Russia launch another assault), are strong enough to win and are backed by a credible nuclear deterrent.

There are so far no signs that the Europeans are up for that. For all the talk of supporting Ukraine, no Europeans have suggested that preventing Ukraine falling once again under Moscow's rule is worth a nuclear war. Macron's frank statement that Ukraine's security was not vital enough for France to use its nuclear weapons there made this crystal clear. So, unless Ukraine gets nuclear weapons of its own, there is a real chance that Trump's callously offhand comment that "Ukraine might not survive" might prove to be prophetic. This is the way things go in our hard new world.

The Europeans are more likely to make a united stand on Ukraine's border with Poland, because that is the point at which the Germans start to feel very directly threatened. But the Poles will be nervous about taking that for granted, remembering how often in the past their Western neighbours have allowed Russia's sphere to extend all the way to the Vistula River and beyond. Would other Europeans really decide that preventing Poland falling once again under Moscow's shadow was worth the risk of nuclear war?

What about the Baltics, or Finland? When the Baltics joined NATO, no one – except of course the Baltics themselves – took seriously the idea that Russia might one day threaten them. When Finland and Sweden were admitted, everyone assumed that Russia's assault on Ukraine would be easy to defeat. Now everyone knows better. If and when these front-line states face a real threat, the mere fact of NATO membership will do little to determine how other Europeans respond. They will ask whether saving them from Russia is vital enough to their own security to risk a nuclear war. I wouldn't bet the answer will be "yes." Europe has some big questions to ponder. And so do the rest of us, because there is much we can learn from Europe's present about Asia's future.

People complain that Donald Trump's approach to alliances is transactional. But all alliances are transactional when the chips are down, when the costs are real and the risks potentially huge. Countries only ever make those choices to support *another* country's security when their *own* vital interests demand it. If you doubt that, ask any Ukrainian. Or find an Australian who remembers the Fall of Singapore in 1942. We understand nothing about Australia's alliance with America if we do not understand this.

America has an alliance with Australia because it serves America's strategic position in our region. If America's interests change and it no longer wants to maintain that position, then the alliance with Australia will no longer be needed and it will wither away, just as our alliance with Britain swiftly withered after it pulled out of Asia. So whether we can rely on America to keep us secure in future depends above all on whether it is serious about staying as a major strategic power in Asia. And this is bad news, because America's position in Asia today is more precarious than at any time since the late nineteenth century.

That is because in Asia today America faces by far the most formidable strategic rival it has ever confronted. It is not just GDP. Today China equals or eclipses America at the leading edge of a host of key technologies, including AI and electric vehicles, and its growing armed forces have eliminated America's former decisive superiority in maritime warfare in the Western Pacific. This changes everything, fundamentally.

China's aim is clear. Like Russia, it wants to take its place alongside America in the top tier of a multipolar order. To do that it must push America out of East Asia and the Western Pacific. The big question is how America responds. Superficially, it seems that America is determined to push back and resist China's challenge. When the scale of Beijing's ambition was first clearly acknowledged in Trump's first term, China was immediately labelled America's most serious strategic rival. Suddenly everyone in Washington agreed on this. Amid talk of a "new Cold War," there was rare consensus across the political divide that China must be countered and contained. Joe Biden took office in 2021 promising to win what he called the "contest for the twenty-first century" against China.

But it has never been that simple, for two reasons. First, the strategic aim has been mixed up with economic and technological concerns. Americans across the political spectrum were determined to shield American companies and workers from Chinese competition, and to stop China taking the lead on new technologies. These different agendas were clearly related and it was easy to get them mixed up, so that politicians and commentators talking tough on trade and technological issues sounded as if they were equally serious about winning the contest with China over strategic leadership in Asia.

That was not always true, especially when it comes to Trump himself. He has always been obsessed with China as an economic rival and a threat to America's social cohesion. He accuses the Chinese of stealing American jobs and technology, thus destroying US manufacturing, and even of fomenting its social problems. He remains fixated on China's trade surplus with America, making it the primary target of his tariff frenzy. But there is no evidence that Trump cares much, if at all, about the strategic contest with China in Asia. On the contrary, a lot of evidence points the other way. It suggests that Trump is happy to deal with China in the same way he deals with Russia, as a fellow great power in a multipolar world. That means conceding China's right to an exclusive sphere of influence in its own backyard, just as he insists on America's right to dominate the Western Hemisphere.

So, on strategic questions, Trump really isn't a China hawk. He likes and respects Xi Jinping and admires China's achievements. Consider these quotes from Trump last year, collected by Graham Allison of Harvard: "I respect China." "I very much respect President Xi." "President Xi is brilliant. The press hates it when I call President Xi brilliant, but well, he's a brilliant guy." "I want China to do great. I do." "I love China." Can you imagine Trump saying that about Japan, South Korea or Taiwan? He dislikes America's Asian allies and has often dismissed the idea that America should defend Taiwan.

And he is not alone. Trump has appointed few mainstream China hawks to senior jobs. One of those few, former national security advisor Mike Waltz, has already been moved on. Most of his team, including Director of National Intelligence Tulsi Gabbard and Pete Hegseth at the Pentagon, are much closer to Trump's view than to the old Washington consensus. Most important, however, is the fact that Trump himself does not speak of China as a strategic rival but only as an economic one. And this fits with the way he has long seen America's place in the world, and the way he has dealt with Europe. Republican China hawks imagine that Trump has deserted Ukraine, abandoned Europe and courted Putin so that he can focus on defeating China to defend US regional and global leadership. But Trump has never believed that any of that really matters for America.

Trump's attitude and his team's divisions, plus their all-pervasive incompetence, mean there will be no clear leadership from this administration to guide and focus an effective US response to China's challenge. Those who hope that America will be pushing back effectively against China over the next few years will be disappointed.

But Trump's accommodating attitude to China's strategic ambitions doesn't mean that the danger of escalating strategic rivalry between the world's two strongest states has disappeared. On the contrary there remains a real risk that, whatever Trump may wish or intend, events may well conspire to create crises that take on a life of their own and spiral out of control. How likely that is will depend in part on Beijing. The more provocatively it behaves over the next few years, the more likely a serious crisis is. But that in turn will depend on how Washington behaves under Trump. However relaxed he may be about China's plans for Asia, his wild assaults on China's trade and economic interests must raise tempers and shorten fuses in Beijing. And we can be sure that any crisis that does flare up will be woefully mismanaged. So there is nothing reassuring about the new administration's China policy.

The second reason why US allies have been misled by Washington's reassuring talk of resolve to defeat China's challenge is that the talk has not been followed by any effective action. This is evident from the Biden administration's record. On the one hand, their initial perception of China's challenge was stark. In a much-feted book published in 2012, one of Biden's senior officials, Rush Doshi, wrote of China not just seeking greater influence in its own region but "seeking to shape the twenty-first century, much as the US shaped the twentieth." They believed that China planned to take America's place not just as the leading power in East Asia but as the leading power globally. Hence Biden's talk of winning the twenty-first century. They were still talking this way in 2024. Biden's would-be successor, Kamala Harris, promised the Democratic Convention that she would ensure "that America, not China, wins the competition for the twenty-first century, and that we strengthen, not abdicate, our global leadership."

All this suggested that the Biden team thought China posed a potential existential threat to America. Like the rivals that had seemed poised to dominate Eurasia in the twentieth century, China had to be blocked from hegemony in East Asia and the Western Pacific, lest it go on from there to become a Eurasian hegemon with the power to threaten America at home in the Western Hemisphere.

At the very same time, many prominent players in Washington believed that America did not need to do much to defeat China's challenge. It needed only stand back and hold the line until China either collapsed or came to its senses and accepted US primacy. And the Biden team also stressed their determination to ensure the rivalry did not get too dangerous or too costly. They wanted to stand up to China and defeat its challenge while "responsibly managing competition." They never explained how they thought they could "manage" competition with China while refusing to accommodate any of its ambitions. They apparently just assumed that China would be content to let those ambitions go without a fight. That really was a delusion.

More modest US aims in Asia would have been more compatible with "managed competition." Washington could take a half-step back. America would stay in Asia, not to dominate the region but only to balance China and stop it dominating. Jake Sullivan and Kurt Campbell, who became Biden's China supremo, argued this way in an essay published shortly before Biden took office.

This is a very appealing idea. In fact, it is an approach to America's future in Asia that I proposed fifteen years ago in my first Quarterly Essay, *Power Shift*, and in a subsequent book, *The China Choice*. If the Biden team had been serious about "responsibly managing competition" with China, this is the approach they would have taken. But there are two big problems. First, there was no longer any reason to think that China would settle for this kind of power-sharing deal in Asia. Second, everyone in Washington baulks at the idea. As I found when I went around the town talking about *The China Choice*, no one there is really willing to entertain the idea of sharing power with China as an equal. China's challenge is seen in Manichean terms, and no one anywhere near public office is willing to argue for a policy of accommodation. That left them no option but to launch a full-scale military, economic and diplomatic campaign to compel Beijing to accept America's terms. And at the same time to sweet-talk Beijing so that the rivalry didn't get out of hand. That was a big task, considering that China is by far the most formidable rival America has ever faced, and notoriously resistant to sweet talk.

Not surprisingly, the Biden administration completely failed in both parts of the task they set for themselves. Instead of sweet talk, diplomacy with Beijing was dominated by a series of avoidable contretemps. These included the needlessly acrimonious initial meeting between senior officials in Anchorage in 2021, Nancy Pelosi's pointlessly provocative visit to Taiwan in 2022, and the comic-opera kerfuffle over the Chinese spy balloon in 2023. These missteps played out alongside steadily escalating initiatives to block Chinese exports to America and Chinese access to US technology. There was no serious effort to engage China in a dialogue about the long-term trajectory of their relationship, because the determination to perpetuate US primacy left nothing to discuss.

So instead of engaging China, the Biden administration talked up action on hot-button domestic issues as the key to "outcompeting" China. This was a big part of the pitch for Biden's biggest initiatives, the *CHIPS and Science Act* and the *Inflation Reduction Act*. Americans were encouraged to think that the contest for the twenty-first century could be won for next to nothing, simply by doing things at home in America that they wanted to do anyway. But that meant Biden's promise to outcompete China went unfulfilled. For example, to compete with Beijing for influence in East Asia, Washington had to reclaim its place as a key economic partner for regional countries. But that meant reopening the US market to the region's exports, and no one was willing to do that against the protectionist tide in US politics.

This meant there was very little that Biden actually did. His signature policies in Asia were the Quad and AUKUS, name-checked in every speech and press conference. It is hard to overstate how insignificant these initiatives are compared to the scale of the task Biden had set himself in containing China. The Quad, for example, is supposed to demonstrate the shared resolve of Japan, India and Australia to back America to the hilt against Beijing. But there is nothing to it but a series of meetings which gingerly avoid talking about China or what they might do about it. AUKUS was supposed to highlight the three partners' determination to deter China from its challenge, by possibly providing Australia with a small fleet of nuclear-powered submarines twenty-five years from now. Even if it worked, that wouldn't change the military balance in Asia. It does nothing to help America win the contest with China that is already well underway.

*

In fact, none of these things really matter much to America's contest with China. What really counts is the balance of military power and resolve. That is because the stakes are so high, especially for the Chinese. For them it is about escaping subordination to US power and claiming what they see as their rightful place as America's equal. For America, it is about resisting China's claims to equality and preserving America's place at the apex of global power.

Great powers are usually reluctant to go to war with one another, because such wars are so dangerous and costly. But throughout history, contests like these about countries' places in the international power hierarchy are exactly what have driven great powers to fight. That does not make war inevitable, because it is always possible that one side or both decide to avoid war by making concessions. But it does mean that the possibility of war overshadows the entire contest.

This is what we are seeing in Asia, as in Ukraine. The rivalry between America and China is playing out primarily as a test of their relative military power and resolve over "flashpoints" in the South China Sea, the East China Sea and, above all, Taiwan. If the Chinese attack Taiwan, either by invasion or blockade, Washington would have to choose between abandoning Taiwan and going to war. If it abandons Taiwan, its entire position in East Asia will be severely, and perhaps fatally, damaged.

The foundation of that position is America's alliances with Japan, South Korea and Australia. The alliance with Japan is by far the most important, and it depends ultimately on Tokyo's confidence that America would be willing and able to defend it from China. Even small doubts about that would raise big questions in Tokyo about whether the alliance still makes sense for them. That makes the alliance more fragile than it appears. Like the Europeans, the Japanese would love to keep relying on America, but they can see where things are heading. It is clear in Tokyo that the more powerful China becomes, the more it would cost America to defend Japan from a Chinese attack, and the more likely it therefore becomes that America would let Japan down by deciding not to.

Those doubts would quickly grow if America failed to defend Taiwan. The Japanese would sooner or later – and probably quite soon – decide to go their own way. That is not hard for Japan to do by expanding its armed forces and building nuclear weapons. Then America would lose the Japanese bases which are essential for its military operations in the Western Pacific, and the prestige that comes from its role as Japan's protector. US standing elsewhere in the region would crash, and China would be a big step closer to getting America out of East Asia. This is all clearly understood by leaders in Beijing, which is why they are so tempted to attack Taiwan.

It is also clearly understood in Washington. They know that failing to defend Taiwan would be fatal to the US position in Asia, but they definitely do not want a war with China, so for them everything depends on convincing the Chinese that they would defend Taiwan. It is no exaggeration to say that America's strategic future in Asia depends on its success at doing this.

Taiwan is not the only testing ground for US resolve. The dispute over the reefs and atolls between China and the Philippines is another. America's credibility would be at stake if one of the frequent incidents there escalated into conflict between Chinese and Philippine military forces. Washington would then have to choose between undermining its credibility by abandoning its ally or risking a clash with China that could well escalate into full-scale war over an uninhabited atoll. That is a choice that Washington desperately wants to avoid. And again, avoiding it depends on convincing Beijing that America would fight.

These flashpoints are where the rubber meets the road in Asia's strategic rivalry. Neither side wants war, but each side wants to convince the other that it is willing to fight to achieve its aims.

The critical question for Australians, as we wonder whether America will be here for us in the decades ahead, is whether Washington is doing enough to convince Beijing that it is really willing to go to war to defend America's position in Asia.

America's response to the invasion of Ukraine has a bearing on this. In the first optimistic months after Russia invaded, many people thought that America's hand against China had been strengthened. They hoped that Russia's early failures and Ukraine's heroic defence would discourage Beijing from trying to take Taiwan by force. They thought the Chinese would be surprised and alarmed by the broad international support for Ukraine and the tough sanctions imposed on Russia. And they hoped that Washington's leadership of the international response had restored its credibility and affirmed its resolve to defend the US-led global order.

That all looks very different now. Even before Trump returned to the White House, the key message that Beijing took from the whole tragedy is that America is not willing to fight Russia to defend Ukraine. If that is so when its strategic leadership in Europe and the credibility of US global leadership is at stake, why would it fight China to defend Taiwan and its position in Asia? It is not an easy question for Washington to answer.

It looks even harder to answer when we consider what Washington has actually done in recent years to convince Beijing of its resolve. One thing it has done is turn up the rhetoric. After decades of artful ambiguity from Washington, Biden repeatedly said quite categorically that America would defend Taiwan if China attacked. He likewise went further than his predecessors by repeatedly declaring his "ironclad" commitment to support Manila militarily in a conflict with China over the disputed reefs and atolls. Trump's language is very different. He has often spoken dismissively of Taiwan and questioned whether America can defend it or needs to. Even the most impressive of Trump's strategic advisers, noted China hawk Elbridge Colby, has acknowledged that defending Taiwan is not an existential imperative for America.

But effective deterrence depends more on what is actually done than on what is said. The best way to convince an adversary that you are willing to fight is to have clearly equipped yourself to fight and win. Conversely, it is hard to convey your resolve to fight if you haven't taken those necessary steps. This is America's situation in Asia today.

There is something bewildering about what has happened to America's military position in Asia. It is now almost thirty years since America and China last came close to a serious military confrontation over Taiwan. Back then, America's air and naval forces were incomparably superior to China's. If it had come to blows, the outcome was not in doubt, so Beijing backed down. But since then the maritime military balance has been overturned. China's economic growth and technological development have underwritten massive investments in advanced air and naval forces. They have been designed specifically to prevent America projecting military power into the Western Pacific. These new capabilities reinforce the inherent advantages that China already enjoys from operating close to home and fighting on the defensive, which, in the current era of maritime warfare, is much easier than offence.

And yet America has done virtually nothing in response. While China's maritime forces have grown exponentially in size and sophistication, US military strength in the Western Pacific has hardly increased at all. America's previously decisive advantage has collapsed. It is widely understood in Washington, including by Colby, that there is now no serious chance that America can defend Taiwan from China. This conclusion is backed by a number of recent and highly credible war games.

And then there are China's nuclear weapons. Until just a few years ago, US policymakers downplayed China's nuclear forces because they were small and relatively unsophisticated. Just six years ago, Jake Sullivan and Kurt Campbell could confidently say that, "the kind of nuclear brinkmanship that took place over Berlin and Cuba has no corollary in US–China ties."

These illusions have been shattered by evidence that China is quickly building a lot more nuclear weapons. The Pentagon now estimates that China's arsenal will grow from around 400 warheads to 1000 by 2030 and 1500 by 2035. It is also building a lot more intercontinental ballistic missiles capable of hitting US cities. This has taken US strategic planners by surprise. Suddenly there is a lot of talk in Washington about how to respond. Many argue that to maintain adequate deterrence America must expand its own nuclear forces for the first time since the end of the Cold War. But this misses the key weakness in America's position. The problem is not that America has too few nuclear weapons. What it lacks is the clear resolve to use them.

To see what this would mean in practice, think about what would happen if China attacked Taiwan and America did decide to go to war in Taiwan's defence. The conflict would quickly escalate into a very intense and highly destructive conventional – non-nuclear – air and naval war, with massive losses on both sides. After a few weeks, if not before, it would be clear to both Beijing and Washington that neither had any chance of winning this kind of war. Neither side could inflict enough damage to compel the other to back off, especially after they had lost so much. So both sides would soon consider using nuclear threats.

Everything would then depend on whose threats were more credible, given the risk that any nuclear exchange could so easily escalate to massive attacks on both sides' homelands. To resist Chinese nuclear blackmail, Washington must convince Beijing that it would retaliate with nuclear weapons, even though that would very likely lead to Chinese nuclear counterattacks on America itself. It is hard to see how America can do that, for the same reason that America could not convince Moscow that it was willing to fight a nuclear war over Ukraine. As we have seen, in the Cold War, Washington convinced Moscow of its nuclear resolve by massive spending on forward-deployed conventional forces and vast nuclear forces, creating new and unprecedented strategic alliances and making explicit public statements that it accepted the possibility of nuclear attack as the price of containing its rival. All this was backed by a credible, clearly articulated and widely accepted account of precisely why containing the Soviets was vital to US security. Washington has done none of these things today in Asia. It has allowed its conventional force advantage to disappear. It sticks to longstanding alliances from habit rather than to serve contemporary strategic imperatives. It has never clearly explained what those imperatives are. And since China emerged as a strategic rival, no US leader has suggested to the American people that containing China's ambitions in East Asia was so important that it might mean nuclear attacks on US cities.

All this makes it very hard for Washington to neutralise Chinese nuclear threats with credible counterthreats of nuclear retaliation. That in turn makes it much easier for the Chinese to convince the Americans to back off. The more clearly Chinese leaders understand this, the more likely they are to risk putting US resolve to the test by attacking Taiwan. And the more clearly US leaders understand this – and we had better hope they do – the more likely they are to fail that test by abandoning Taiwan, just as both Biden and Trump have, in their different ways, abandoned Ukraine.

It is hard to escape the conclusion that the US policy elite have been very muddled about China for a long time. They have both exaggerated China's power and underestimated it at the same. They have feared that China is becoming strong enough to dominate the world and threaten America itself, while at the same time assuming it would be easy to confront and contain it. It is a pattern common to many strategic failures. We often *overestimate* the threat posed by an adversary by mistakenly seeing our most vital interests at stake – and then we *underestimate* what it will cost to deal with it. So we blunder into a needless rivalry or conflict, which we find we can't win, and then realise we don't need to win anyway. That is what happened in Vietnam, Iraq, Afghanistan – and Ukraine. But the costs of repeating this mistake now in Asia are far higher. They could be catastrophic.

Washington's instinct to resist China is driven by the assumption that if it is allowed to dominate East Asia and the Western Pacific it will go on to dominate Eurasia and thus become strong enough to threaten America itself. It is an assumption encapsulated in former defence secretary Lloyd Austin's remark that "the United States can be secure only if Asia is secure." But the claim does not withstand scrutiny. There is no reason to believe that China will be strong enough to extend its primacy beyond East Asia and the Western Pacific. It will not be able to dominate Asia as a whole, because India stands in its way. India is still a rising power, but it is formidable already and will be more formidable still in future, and it is determined not to live in China's shadow.

Nor, as we have seen, will China be able to dominate Russia, despite its greater power. That partnership today serves a shared aim to replace the US-led unipolar order with a multipolar global order in which they have key roles, and to exclude America from their respective spheres of influence. But Ukraine has taught us that nothing matters more to Russia than to assert its place as a great power in its own right, and that its nuclear weapons give it a potent capacity to do so. And it will not be alone. If China comes to dominate East Asia and then tries to extend its sway over Eurasia as a whole, the most likely outcome by far would be for India, Russia and Europe to act together to resist it. And if they seemed unequal to the task, America could and no doubt would then intervene, throwing its weight behind China's rivals to strengthen the balance of power – as it has done before.

The fact is that the "balance of power" principle really works to stop any single great power dominating all the others. Throughout history, in any group of great powers the weaker members have banded together to prevent the strongest from dominating them all. That is what happened in Europe repeatedly, as shifting coalitions formed and reformed to defeat successive Spanish,

French, German and Russian attempts to dominate the continent. It is happening again today, as China and Russia align to resist US global hegemony. It will prevent China dominating Eurasia and seriously threatening America. There is always a price, of course, paid by the small and middle powers that get caught up in great-power rivalries, as Ukraine and Taiwan show. But it means that America does not have a truly vital interest in preventing China from replacing it as the leading power in East Asia and the Western Pacific. Instead, China, like America, is destined to operate within a global multipolar order in which both will be able to flourish if they are content to accept it.

This multipolar world of regional great powers is the new reality that Australia must learn to live with, and, thanks to Trump, it is coming at us faster than ever. Unless a catastrophic crisis intervenes, he will accelerate America's departure from Asia and shift the Washington consensus towards accepting that. By the end of his second term, one wonders whether any serious player in Washington will still be arguing that America must remain the primary power in East Asia. The Republican Party already, it seems, accepts Trump's view of everything. The Democratic Party faces a daunting task to completely reinvent itself to compete in Trump's America. The foreign policy assumptions of the old Clinton/Biden era cannot survive that process. American voters, it seems, want leaders who look and sound strong but have no appetite for the costs and risks of global leadership. Trump gives them exactly what they want, and the Democrats will have to emulate him if they want to defeat his movement.

China, meanwhile, will face an interesting choice. On the one hand, Trump's evident reluctance to get dragged into confrontations over Taiwan or the South China Sea might tempt Beijing to bring on a crisis, hoping that by refusing to intervene Trump would finally destroy US credibility and bring the American era in Asia to a swift conclusion. On the other hand, with trends going their way Chinese leaders may well decide that their best course is to sit back and wait for events to take their natural course. The way things are going, they won't have to wait long.

In fact, the final nudge that brings the American era in Asia to a close may not come from China at all, but from Korea. When Obama handed over the

Oval Office to Trump in 2017, he warned his successor that the most serious problem he would face was North Korea's nuclear capability. But Trump was no more successful than his predecessors in stopping this, so the whole subject was allowed to slip quietly off Washington's agenda. Under Biden it hardly got a mention, while Pyongyang's nuclear and missiles forces steadily grew. North Korea now has the capacity to launch nuclear attacks not just on its Asian neighbours but on American cities. Of course there is no real threat of an unprovoked attack on America itself, because America could mount such devastating retaliation. But the North's intercontinental nuclear capacity poses an acute problem for Seoul.

South Korea has in the past been reassured that the North would never mount a nuclear attack against it for fear of US retaliation. But everything changes when the potential aggressor can attack America itself. That raises the stakes for Washington enormously and makes it much less certain that Washington would follow through on its deterrent threat. And that in turn makes Seoul much less confident that US threats would deter a North Korean nuclear attack, making it acutely vulnerable to North Korean nuclear blackmail.

Seoul has tried to ease these fears by seeking extra reassurance from Washington, but when President Yoon Suk Yeol went to Washington for a high-profile summit with Biden in 2024, he was palmed off with much weaker measures than he had hoped for. The result, inevitably, is that there is now serious discussion in Seoul about the need for South Korea to get nuclear weapons of its own. Trump's open hostility to US allies – especially South Korea, it seems – will make the need feel more urgent still. If Seoul takes this step, or even puts it more squarely on the table, the effect on America's position in Asia would be dramatic. It is not just that the US alliance with South Korea would probably collapse. Tokyo would also face big questions. It faces the same risks from North Korea as the South does, and they amplify the bigger doubts about America's long-term commitment to defend Japan from China. If Japan went nuclear, the rationale for maintaining its US alliance would crumble, and with it America's strategic place in Asia. Beijing would have won the contest with America without fighting, as Sun

Tzu enjoins. And in Washington there might well be a quiet sigh of relief.

What will that mean for Asia? Those most committed to America staying paint the darkest picture of what happens after this. They foresee a region crushed under the brutal heel of Chinese military and economic domination, like Eastern Europe under Stalin or Asia under Imperial Japan. That is not impossible, and we should bear it in mind as we plan for our future in the new Asia, because worst-case scenarios have a place in policymaking. But it is far from the only outcome, or the most likely, and to focus too much on the gloomiest predictions will make it harder for us to make the best of things as they unfold. How might that look?

The first thing to be clear about is that China will be the strongest power in East Asia and the Western Pacific by a very long way. Its closest competitor will be India, but neither China nor India will be strong enough to compete effectively in the other's backyard. Their rivalry will therefore be limited to jockeying for position along the boundary between their respective spheres of influence. This will ensure that countries lying along that boundary, including Australia, will have options to use each of these great powers as a counterbalance and shield against the other.

Japan will not function as a great power in this East Asia, but it will remain easily strong enough to maintain a high degree of independence within the Chinese-led order, and that alone will make it harder for China to impose itself too heavy-handedly on the region. As Indonesia rises to take its place as the world's fourth-biggest economy, it will have the potential to exercise real strategic weight, and could do the same. Other major regional countries – Vietnam, South Korea, perhaps Thailand and Singapore – will also be strong enough at least to deflect or modulate the way China uses its power – and of course they will have strong incentives to cooperate to do so.

We will thus find ourselves not just in a multipolar world but in a multipolar Asia, divided between two great powers and with a number of influential middle powers too. This is the region in which Australia should be preparing to make its way. We should start by recognising that Asia's future, and Australia's, will not be decided in Washington. It will be decided in Asia.

THE END OF THE WORLD AS WE KNOW IT

It was five years ago that Scott Morrison first declared the rise of great-power rivalry had made Australia's strategic circumstances more threatening than at any time since World War II. Since then, his warning, endlessly and eagerly repeated, has been accepted as incontrovertible. It makes for good politics, of course. Leaders like to present themselves as boldly confronting dire threats on our behalf. But this startling and alarming assessment has not disturbed the fundamentally optimistic assumptions that still frame Australia's defence and foreign policies. Indeed, both the Morrison and Albanese governments have been distinctly upbeat. They have conveyed the impression that China's and Russia's challenges to the international order have been met with clarity, resolve and unity by America and its allies. The way they describe it, like-minded countries across the world from Finland to New Zealand have recognised the seriousness of the threat and resolved to resist it together. They proudly say that Australia has played its part through AUKUS and the Quad, by getting closer to Japan, deepening relations with our region and forging partnerships with an expanding NATO.

So the working assumption in Canberra has been that, despite the looming dangers, everything will turn out well. Russia's invasion of Ukraine will be decisively defeated. Chinese aggression towards Taiwan will be deterred. America's place as the world's primary power and guardian of the international order will be preserved. And Australia's alliance with America will grow even stronger. This is why neither side of politics has matched their dire warnings with the serious defence and foreign policy responses needed if all this optimism turns out to be misplaced. They have not addressed the very real risk that America and China will go to war over an issue like Taiwan, with catastrophic consequences for everyone. Nor have they begun to prepare for the very high likelihood that, with or without a war, America will soon withdraw from Asia.

That is why, in a strange, sad way, Donald Trump is doing us a favour by puncturing this complacent optimism, making brutally clear the strategic realities that the Biden team's delusions helped our governments ignore. The big question is how the returned Albanese government responds. Its instinct and preference will be to cling to the assumption that the foundations of our alliance remain strong, and to see Trump himself as the problem. It will tend to think the job is simply to manage Trump, shielding the alliance from his whims so that it can emerge unscathed when normality returns after he goes.

That would be a big mistake, as the strategic crises in Europe and Asia make clear. Perhaps, with Trump in the White House, the risk of war between America and China, though still very real, has gone down. But that is only because America's withdrawal from Asia has accelerated. That makes it even more urgent now for Australia to work out how to make our way, for the first time in our history, in an Asia no longer made safe for us by a great and powerful friend.

*

The first Albanese government's foreign and defence policies could not have been further from meeting this responsibility. They have been modest to a fault, even timid. That is partly a matter of politics: they were determined to deny the Coalition any targets in areas where they feel inherently vulnerable. But it was also, I think, that no one in the government had the imagination to see what was happening or the energy to respond.

Their best achievement was to reset relations with Beijing after the spectacular falling-out under Scott Morrison. This was important, and Penny Wong managed it well. But it wasn't hard because Beijing was also keen to get things back on track, so she was pushing on an open door. Otherwise, Labor's agenda was dominated by AUKUS. Albanese's fateful decision to adopt Morrison's policy as his own overshadowed his government's entire foreign and defence policies. It locked them into unconditional support for the Biden administration's dream of containing China, which was precisely what Biden's people intended AUKUS to do. As one of its principal US architects, Biden's national security advisor, Jake Sullivan, recently said,

AUKUS is "a strategic marriage between the United States and Australia for half a century."

Only one person in the Albanese cabinet seems to have thought that there might be more to do than support Washington's dream of perpetual primacy. Wong occasionally conjured a different vision. In some of her speeches she hinted that America should step back to a balancing role in Asia. As we have seen, this is an appealing idea that would serve Australia well, easing US–China tensions while setting some limits to China's power. But, as we have also seen, the idea has little appeal in Washington and none at all in Beijing. Wong knows that, so her musings were most likely designed to appeal to Southeast Asian audiences who are anxious that America's hopes to retain primacy are fuelling dangerous rivalry. There is certainly no evidence that she ever tried seriously to convince either her colleagues in Canberra or her counterparts in Washington to consider it.

Instead, Labor has focused both its defence and foreign policies on the hope that US primacy can be preserved. It is striking how little it has achieved. In defence, it has given priority to developing forces to support America in a war with China. It is an "America First" policy. The keystone is the AUKUS plan to buy nuclear-powered submarines (SSNs). The idea is that a fleet of Australian SSNs would help America deter China from the kind of military challenge – over Taiwan or in the South China Sea – that, as we explored earlier, would present Washington with an impossible choice between abandoning its position in Asia or going to war with China.

There are many reasons why this approach will not work. First, it is too slow. Even if the submarines are delivered as planned, Australia's SSNs would not add to the combined US and allied submarine capabilities in the Pacific for at least twenty years, whereas China needs deterring over the next decade. During the 2030s, AUKUS will actually reduce US capacity rather than increase it, as Virginia-class subs are diverted from the highly experienced US Navy to a Royal Australian Navy still struggling to operate them.

Second, it is too small. China will not be reliably deterred unless US forces in the Western Pacific are massively increased. By the time they arrive, if they ever do, eight Australian SSNs will do almost nothing to improve America's chances of winning a US–China war, and thus nothing to help America deter Chinese aggression.

Third, the AUKUS subs are not clearly committed to the fight. America seems to take it for granted that they are, but Canberra says they are not. That muddle undermines any deterrent value they might have. The essence of deterrence is to convince the adversary that you have both the capacity and the resolve to go to war. So the Chinese need to believe Australia is seriously committed to sending SSNs to war against China. Washington certainly expects we would, but Canberra refuses to say. That makes it easy for Beijing to dismiss them. If Canberra's leaders were serious about helping to deter Beijing, they would unambiguously commit to send our forces, just as America's NATO allies were unambiguously committed to support one another in the Cold War. It is clear why they don't take that step, though. They don't want to alarm Australians or anger Beijing.

Fourth, and most important, it is futile for Australia to frame its defence around US deterrence of China when America itself is not serious about it. America will not be able to deter China's challenge unless and until Washington can convince Beijing that it is willing to fight a nuclear war to remain Asia's primary power, and as we have seen, there has been no sign of that. Nonetheless, some of the things that have been done recently under the AUKUS umbrella have increased the risk that Australia would be embroiled in a US–China war if one broke out.

US investments in facilities to support US Air Force long-range strike missions from Tindal in the Northern Territory make no serious difference to America's capacity to deter or win a war with China. But they mark a significant step in preparations for Australia to support America in such a war. There can be no doubt that America confidently expects Canberra's agreement to use these facilities if it comes to war, and it is at least quite likely that the missions flown from Tindal against targets in China would involve nuclear strikes. Our "strategic marriage" to America under AUKUS makes it practically impossible to refuse US requests for this kind of support, and we cannot assume that there will not be more of them in the years ahead. China hawks in the administration will be eagerly pressing US allies to do more, and Trump will give them a free hand. It is classic Trump to expect more and more from allies while he offers them less and less. This is the dead end into which our "America First" defence policy has led us.

We've had an "America First" foreign policy too. It is sobering to see how narrowly directed our diplomacy now is to supporting the US. Compare the agenda today with the achievements of the 1980s and 1990s, when Australia did a lot to shape the international order, solve difficult problems and serve a wide range of interests. The Cairns Group and APEC, the Cambodian Peace Agreements, the Chemical Weapons Convention, the Comprehensive Nuclear Test Ban Treaty, the South Pacific Nuclear Free Zone, our promotion of the ASEAN Regional Forum, the Antarctic Mining Ban, sanctions on South Africa to end apartheid, our role in East Timor's transition to independence, and many more. This built on earlier achievements, including H.V. Evatt's role in creating the United Nations, Percy Spender's initiatives in creating ANZUS and the Colombo Plan, and Gough Whitlam's daring diplomacy with China.

And today? Apart from resuming contact with Beijing, the big item on the Labor agenda has been deepening engagement with our neighbours in the South Pacific and Southeast Asia. But in both regions the primary aim has been to urge our neighbours to side with America against China. In the South Pacific, there was the deal with Tuvalu to allow Tuvaluans to migrate to Australia to escape the consequences of climate change in exchange for granting Australia a veto over security arrangements with China. There was the deal with Papua New Guinea under which Australia committed $600 million to fund a PNG team in the NRL, in return for which Port Moresby promised to limit China's security role in PNG. There was the $400-million region-wide Pacific Policing Initiative, aimed at pre-empting Chinese efforts to build a bigger role in regional security affairs. And several more, all wrapped up in transparently hypocritical talk of Australia's altruistic concerns for our "Pacific Family."

Canberra is clinging to the old assumption, dating back to the nineteenth century, that Australia must try to keep any country other than our closest allies out of our backyard. It is our own idea of an exclusive sphere of influence. This has intuitive appeal: it makes sense to keep potential enemies far from our shores. But China is too big to be kept out of our region. It has too much to offer our island neighbours for them to turn their backs, just as China has too much to offer Australia for us to turn our back.

For the South Pacific countries, the rise of China is the biggest shift in their international circumstances since they became independent in the 1970s and 1980s. They must work out how to make their way in a region no longer dominated by a distant and often neglectful but relatively benign United States. Like us, they are going to have to learn to live with Chinese power and influence, carefully balancing their need to engage with their need not to be overwhelmed. It is an immense task, and we are not helping. In fact, we are making it harder by trying to force on them an approach they know to be oversimplified and certain to fail.

The same applies in Southeast Asia. Despite our new defence agreement with Indonesia, it is absolutely clear that Indonesia continues to see the US–China contest very differently from the way we do. Evan Laksmana, one of Indonesia's most respected strategic analysts, has written that, for many reasons, "Indonesia is unlikely to view the United States as a benevolent provider of regional security in the way Australia does."

Malaysia's prime minister, Anwar Ibrahim, was much blunter last year. If America and Australia have problems with China, he said, "They should not impose it upon us. We do not have a problem with China." More broadly, recent surveys by the Lowy Institute and Singapore's Institute of Southeast Asian Studies showed how attitudes in the region are moving towards China – trends which will only be amplified by Donald Trump.

We will not build the relationships we need in the decades ahead by conceiving our relationships entirely as a zero-sum contest between America and China for regional primacy, and especially not by trying to force our neighbours to follow us by siding with America against China. That would be a dumb decision for them for the same reason it is a dumb decision for us – because it is plain that America will not win.

*

What would a different approach look like? The first step is to rethink our two most important relationships. Start with a long hard look at our relationship with China. It is the most important relationship in the world for Australia, and yet our thinking about it remains stuck in the crude two-dimensional box so memorably described by Tony Abbott back in 2014, when he quipped to Angela Merkel that the relationship was based on "fear and greed."

In Abbott's day, greed predominated. Today it is fear. Labor has avoided any deeper analysis by endlessly reciting an evasive sixteen-word formula that goes: "We will cooperate where we can, disagree where we must and engage in our national interests." The purpose of this formula was clear: to pre-empt any suggestion that the Albanese government was too keen to progress the relationship and was not taking the China threat seriously enough. But there is a lot more at stake in our relations with China than these fears. For a start, it remains, as it was in Abbott's day, by far the most important source of future economic opportunities for Australia and for our neighbours. Indeed, its importance for our economic future is only likely to grow as America withdraws from the global trading system.

We might start by clarifying what exactly we fear. The Chinese Navy's transit round Australia in February underlined the seemingly pervasive concern that Australia faces a direct military threat from China. That is exaggerated. But those who dismiss the idea that we might ever face such a threat are wrong too. The reality is a bit more complicated. Something big is changing in our strategic circumstances, which does raise the long-term risk from China, and from other major powers too. But that doesn't mean China poses a direct military threat to Australia now, and how far the risk grows in future depends in part on us.

Thanks to America's regional strategic primacy, Australia has been virtually immune from the threat of direct military attack since the defeat of

Japan in 1945. Now that is changing. In future it will no longer be militarily impossible for China to attack Australia directly. And not just China: other major regional powers, especially India and eventually perhaps Indonesia, will have the potential to launch significant attacks on Australia.

But that does not mean we face now a serious threat of Chinese military attack. Today the only circumstance in which Australia could credibly find itself under attack from China would be if Australia joined America in a war with China over Taiwan. Reports that Australia is a target of Chinese cyber and intelligence operations do not show that Beijing poses a military threat to us, any more than our cyber and intelligence operations targeting China provide evidence that we pose a military threat to them. Certainly the Chinese naval task group posed no serious threat to Australia, because it could have been swiftly destroyed by the ADF if it had shown any serious hostile intent.

It is harder to say whether China might become militarily aggressive towards us in future. We cannot assume that it will from its military build-up alone, because countries often expand their armed forces to defend themselves rather than attack others.

But, equally, we cannot rule out the possibility that China might decide to use armed force against Australia in decades to come. Some aspects of China's naval build-up, especially its sustained investment in aircraft carriers, which would have no useful role in a US–China war over Taiwan, suggest that it wants to be able to conduct long-range power-projection operations, which could encompass Australia. Nonetheless, it does seem unlikely. For one thing, it is a little hard to imagine what China's purpose might be in attacking Australia, given that we are not an easy country to invade. And if we get our defence policy right, it should be possible for us to raise the cost to the point that it is not worth China's while.

This all means that, while we should not ignore it, we should not allow the distant possibility of a Chinese military threat to dominate our thinking about China. There are many other dimensions to what is a very important, complex and ultimately inescapable relationship. It is also a relationship of a completely unfamiliar kind. Other than our two great allies, Australia has never before encountered a country as large, as powerful, as influential in our region, as important to us economically, and with close heritage connections with such a large proportion of our population, as China. Once we abandon the illusion that America is going to manage China for us, we will realise that we have no choice but to find our own way with it. This will not be comfortable or easy. China is ruthless, demanding and completely transactional – though no more than other great powers. Over the past decade, in Canberra and around the country, exaggerated fears and a desire to stay in step with Washington have crowded out serious thinking about China itself and how the very complex range of interests we have in our relationship with it can best be balanced. We have less deep expertise on China now than we had thirty years ago. That has to change.

Our second big task is to rethink our relationship with America. In the decades before the mid-1990s, there was an assumption that – in a Whig-view-of-history way – Australia was gradually but ineluctably emerging from dependence to independence as we left our colonial and imperial past behind and embraced our Asian future. That died away around the time John Howard became prime minister in 1996, when it seemed to many people that the future was America's, and that Australia's future was to become ever more tightly entwined with it, strategically, economically and culturally.

This was the time when a US–Australia free trade agreement seemed both essential and sufficient to guarantee Australia's economic future, and when America's place as the world's dominant military power seemed unchallengeable. The economic illusions of that era were soon overtaken by the hard realities of China's rise, but the strategic illusions have survived. Indeed, they were strengthened by the War on Terror and have been intensified again by the rising fear of China. So we clung on, and stopped imagining we could do anything else.

It is often said, for example, that the intelligence relationship is so close and so important to both sides as to be indissoluble. Don't bet on that. US access to Pine Gap as a location for its satellite ground station is valuable, but very far from essential. Our access to US intelligence under the Five Eyes arrangements is very beneficial and, in some ways, irreplaceable, in that it provides intelligence we could not get in other ways. But that does not mean we could not get by without it. We certainly could.

As things get tough with Washington over the months and years ahead, there will be a temptation to try to placate Donald Trump and earn his favour by meeting his demands for increased defence spending, or by siding with America in its economic war by cutting links with China. There may be good reasons to increase defence spending, but trying to buy Trump's favour is not one of them. Likewise, that futile goal would in no way offset the many powerful arguments against joining a US-led anti-China economic coalition. There are no favours we can do Donald Trump which will keep America strategically engaged in Asia and committed to Australia's defence.

We need to bear these cold realities clearly in mind as we think about our future relations with America. The first step is to recognise that the end of the alliance as we have known it for so long does not mean the end of the relationship. We have been close allies for so long that it is hard to imagine what other form our relationship might take. But with careful management, a new, beneficial post-alliance relationship can evolve, just as our relations with Britain evolved after it withdrew from Asia in the late 1960s. Britain ceased to be an ally, but we continued to have close and productive defence and security links, drawing some strength from our shared history together. Singapore offers another instructive model. It is not a US ally, but it has an excellent relationship with America, including deep defence links. We should aim for a post-alliance relationship like that with America in the years ahead, and we should be building it now. That does not mean severing ties with Washington, but it does mean changing the relationship fundamentally.

Above all, it means acknowledging that the security undertakings in ANZUS can no longer be the foundation of our strategic policy, or of our relationship with America. The Canberra establishment is shocked by any suggestion that we should walk away from the ANZUS commitments. They think we can and must depend on America more than ever in today's hard new world. But that misses the vital point. It is not Australia but America that is walking away from the commitments it made in the ANZUS Treaty in very different circumstances seventy-five years ago. That was plain enough under Joe Biden. It is crystal clear today under Trump. This is the lesson we must draw from Washington's failure to defend Ukraine, from its crumbling position in Asia and from the American voters' decisive rejection of the old idea of US global leadership to which we still cling. Our best path now is to recognise this and start acting accordingly. And we should move quickly to make this clear, because we need to begin right now to build that new post-alliance relationship with America, and we need to start reshaping our armed forces to defend Australia independently.

The place to start is with Taiwan. Through AUKUS and in countless other ways, successive Australian governments have encouraged Washington to believe that it can rely on Canberra's total military support in a war with Beijing over Taiwan. But that is plainly not true. Coalition and Labor governments alike have wilfully avoided seriously considering whether they would send Australia to war with China when Washington calls. It is easy to see why: the question exposes with brutal clarity the fatal weakness of our strategic predicament today. It is unthinkable that Australia would join America in a war that America need not fight, that it cannot win and that would quite possibly become a nuclear war. But as long as we remain convinced that ANZUS is the only possible basis for our security, it is equally unthinkable that we would not join America in that war.

This is not a hypothetical question, because a combination of impatience in Beijing and muddle on Washington means the risk of a US–China war remains very real. Our leaders clearly understand this: that is why they keep saying that our strategic circumstances are more dangerous today than at any time since World War II. If the crisis comes, they will face the most momentous choice any Australian government has ever faced. So it is time to make some decisions. We should break free of the illusion that going to war with China to support America will save our US alliance and make us more secure. We should tell Washington that we will not go to war over Taiwan. We should accept and acknowledge the reality that America will not be keeping Asia safe for us, nor providing an ultimate security guarantee. And we should free ourselves of the debilitating assumption that we cannot look after ourselves.

Our diplomats will find this prospect terrifying, because there is nothing they dislike more than telling Washington things it does not want to hear. But they might have a pleasant surprise in Trump's Washington. He is no fan of America's alliances, and no fan of war with China over Taiwan either. He might warm to a country that lets go of Washington's apron strings and goes its own way.

The defence challenge is bigger. For over fifteen years Australian governments have been talking up the need to expand and reshape our defence forces. So far nothing of value has been achieved. Two successive governments have claimed to be driving major long-term increases in funding. Neither has delivered them. But that debate anyway misses the key point. Australia will need to spend a lot more on defence if it wishes to manage the risk of aggression by a great power like China in the decades ahead, but it is pointless to debate how much more will be needed until we have a much better idea of what exactly we want our forces to do.

The key step is to decide that our armed forces must be designed primarily to defend Australia independently rather than to support America in a war with China. Once that is agreed, it becomes much easier to decide what capabilities we need. One thing that becomes very clear immediately is that we do not need nuclear-powered submarines. A bigger fleet of conventionally powered submarines, much cheaper and less risky to build and operate, plus uncrewed surface and subsurface systems, would be far more cost-effective for defending Australia.

Another thing that becomes clear is that we should be spending far less on surface warships. Today we plan to build the Navy's largest-ever surface fleet, at a time when surface ships are becoming less and less useful in high-intensity maritime warfare because they are becoming so much more vulnerable to aircraft, missiles and submarines. We should be spending the money on those instead.

Finally, the Coalition's commitment to buy another twenty-five F-35 fighters, though less nonsensical than AUKUS and the expanded surface fleet, still raises big questions about our future priorities, for two reasons. First, keeping F-35s operational requires continual support, especially software updates, from the United States. Clearly there are increasing risks in any weapon system that relies on that support continuing. Second, it may not be long before it becomes more effective to use uncrewed drones rather than crewed aircraft for the kinds of missions our fighters will be called upon to perform. It is time we started to shift investment from legacy systems to future capabilities. However, AUKUS is now the overwhelming preoccupation of Defence, at the expense of everything else. Until it is abandoned, it will be impossible for the organisation to begin the real work of transforming our armed forces to meet the demands of a new era.

AUKUS is the perfect symbol of the failure of our entire political system to respond to a changed world. The failure starts at the top. As journalist Shaun Carney has observed, Albanese is patently uneasy whenever questions of foreign and defence policy are raised. Clearly that reflects both a lack of interest and a lack of expertise. But why is that so? He has now led one of our two major parties for six years. Throughout that time, rising strategic rivalry in Asia has been acknowledged by everyone in politics, including Albanese himself, as one of the most pressing issues of our time. He has had plenty of time and opportunity to learn about it all. And yet he still has no capacity even to engage in a serious discussion of the issues. When questioned, his responses remain as scripted, stilted and superficial as ever. It is a major failure, and it has prevented his government from doing anything but follow the misguided tracks laid down by its Coalition predecessors.

But the failures of our political system transcend the shortcomings of individual leaders. The Albanese cabinet has passively acquiesced as the arguments and evidence against AUKUS have mounted up, and the government's defence of it has become correspondingly more threadbare. Have none of them had doubts and thought it their duty to air them? Neither party has generated the lively and urgent internal debate that issues of this magnitude require if good polices are to emerge. Both parties have collaborated to smother the urgent questions we confront beneath a stultifying bipartisanship. Neither side has made any effort to explain to Australians what is happening to our strategic environment or to help them understand the choices we have about how to respond.

There are many reasons for this failure. It is in part a product of the broader decline of mainstream political parties in most Western democracies. But there may be something else at work. I think our political leaders, and their advisers, are frightened of the hard new world we face. They have made their careers in the comfortable world we used to know, and they do not want to take responsibility for guiding Australia into the tougher world ahead. That is why they have taken refuge in complacent assumptions that the old, US-led order will emerge triumphant, leaving the world just as comfortable for us as it seemed to be twenty-five years ago. But if they are wrong to think that is possible, they are also wrong to be so fearful of what is to come. It is going to be difficult for Australia to make its way in the new world that follows the short but easy era of US global primacy. But this is a world we can work with, if we are prepared to face up to its demands.

How to begin? Our biggest problem so far is that we have not acknowledged the way the world is changing. So the first thing we need our leaders to do is to start talking frankly about what is happening and what it means for us. We need them to start delivering speeches that go something like this:

> Australia today faces the biggest shift in our international circumstances since Europeans first settled here in 1788. Over the past few decades, the remarkable economic growth of our Asian neighbours has transformed the global distribution of wealth and power. Today the strongest countries in Asia are among the strongest in the world. China now ranks with America on many dimensions of national power. India is not far behind, and before 2050 Indonesia will have the fourth-biggest economy in the world. That means we live in a multipolar world, and a multipolar Asia.

> In these very different circumstances we cannot expect America to keep playing the same role as hitherto in the security of our region and as Australia's ally. That old order cannot be preserved by war or the threat of war. Our focus instead must be to help create a new order in Asia which fits the new distribution of power and best protects our core national interests, and to do whatever we can to help ensure a peaceful transition from the old order to the new. Then we must prepare Australia to survive and thrive in this new order. That starts by accepting that our relationship with America will change. It will remain an important relationship, but it will become less central to our security in the years to come as America's interests and role in Asia change. We will rely more on our relations with our neighbours to help keep the region peaceful and minimise any threats, and we will rely more on our own forces to defend us from any threats that do arise.
>
> All this will be demanding. The new world we face will be harder than the one we have known for so long. But there is no choice, because the old world we have got used to has gone, and there is no reason to think that we cannot make our way in this new world – as long as we face its challenges squarely.

None of that seems very hard to say. And with a few speeches like this we could start the national conversation we need to have, but which we have so far done our best to avoid.

SOURCES

3 "rock solid": Anthony Albanese quoted in Kate Lyons, "Albanese 'confident' US would come to Australia's defence in event of attack", *Guardian Australia*, 25 February 2025.

3 "is bigger": Penny Wong quoted in Matthew Knott, "Caroline Kennedy calls for 'AUKUS visa' as Canberra braces for election result", *The Sydney Morning Herald*, 4 November 2024.

4 "We are more than allies": Tony Abbott quoted in Paul Osborne and AAP senior political writer, "Abbott says US is 'family'", News.com.au, 18 July 2012.

7 "a mental health condition": Mayo Clinic, "Antisocial personality disorder", Mayo Clinic website, 24 February 2023.

11 "big, beautiful oceans", "far more important": Gabriela Pomeroy and George Wright, "Trump calls Zelensky a 'dictator' as rift between two leaders deepens", BBC News, 20 February 2025.

14 "A power that dominates": Zbigniew Brzezinski, *The Grand Chessboard: American Primacy and its geostrategic imperatives*, Basic Books, New York, 1997, p. 31.

22 "Out of the triumphalism": Marco Rubio, SFRC Confirmation Hearing Opening Remarks, 15 January 2025.

22 "It's not normal": Marco Rubio, interview with Megyn Kelly, *The Megyn Kelly Show*, Washington, DC, 30 January 2025.

24 "Any violence": Tom Stevenson, "Illusions of containment", *London Review of Books*, vol. 47, no. 2, 6 February 2024.

32 "We will not fight": Aaron Blake, "Why Biden and the White House keep talking about World War III", *The Washington Post*, 17 March 2022.

33 "If the territorial": Bob Woodward, *War*, Simon & Schuster, New York, 2024, p. 151ff.

35 "When it comes to": "Anthony Blinken: 'China has been trying to have it both ways'", *The Financial Times*, 3 January 2025.

36 major contribution: Desmond Ball, "Can nuclear war be contained?: Introduction", *The Adelphi Papers*, vol. 21, no. 169, pp. 1–2.

39 US defence spending: Michael E. O'Hanlon, "U.S. Defense Spending in Historical and International Context", The Brookings Institution, 14 May 2024.

40 "rested on the assumption": A.J.P. Taylor, *English History 1914–1945*, Oxford University Press, Oxford, 1965, p. 222.

42 "In 2022 Mr Macron": "Europe thinks the unthinkable on a nuclear bomb", *The Economist*, 12 March 2025.

47 "I respect China", etc.: Graham Allison, "Is Trump a China hawk?" *The Washington Post*, 5 February 2025.

49 "seeking to shape": Rush Doshi, *The Long Game: China's grand strategy to displace American order*, Oxford University Press, Oxford, 2021, p. 2

49 "responsibly managing competition": Jake Sullivan, remarks, Council on Foreign Relations, Washington, DC, 30 January 2024.

55 "the kind of nuclear brinkmanship": Kurt M. Campbell and Jake Sullivan, "Competition without catastrophe: How America can learn to live with China", *Foreign Affairs*, September/October 2019.

55 The Pentagon now estimates: Amrita Jash, "By the numbers: China's nuclear inventory grows", The Lowy Institute, 27 February 2024, lowyinstitute.org/the-interpreter/numbers-china-s-nuclear-inventory-continues-grow, accessed 24 April 2025.

57 "the United States can be secure": Lloyd J. Austin III, 2024 Shangri-La Dialogue, Singapore, 1 June 2024.

63 "a strategic marriage": "Former national security adviser Jake Sullivan: 'The core engines of American power are humming'", *The Financial Times*, 31 January 2025.

66 "Indonesia is unlikely": Evan A. Laksmana, "Embracing the different ways Indonesia and Australia view the region", The Lowy Institute, 20 April 2023, lowyinstitute.org/the-interpreter/embracing-different-ways-indonesia-australia-view-region, accessed 25 April 2025.

66 "They should not": Andrew Tillett, "Don't force your problems with China on us: Malaysian PM's plea", *Australian Financial Review*, 4 March 2024.

66 attitudes in the region are moving towards China: ASEAN Studies Centre at ISEAS – Yusof Ishak Institute, *The State of Southeast Asia 2024: Survey report*, 2 April 2024.

73 Albanese is patently uneasy: Shaun Carney, "Albanese could boldly go where no first-time government has gone before for a century", *The Sydney Morning Herald*, 26 February 2025.

LOSING IT

Correspondence

Patty Kinnersly

Jess Hill's recent Quarterly Essay reflects a frustration that everyone working to prevent and respond to gender-based violence knows all too well: violence against women in Australia is persistent, pervasive and devastating. There are fundamental, chronic failures in many systems – from child protection to youth justice, to police and the courts. There are devastating gaps in the services, support systems and interventions for children, young people and adults, for victims and for those who use violence. Hill's criticism of these failures is legitimate, and these systems need significant reform.

The essay also points to the rise of online misogyny, to a global backlash against gender equality and to readily available harmful pornography, all of which are vastly increasing the challenges we face in responding to violence and sexual assault. I share Hill's deep frustration and her sense of urgency to do more. But this social context means that now is not the time to reduce focus on gender equality and the rights of women – one of the foundation stones of Australia's prevention efforts. Rather, it is a time for us to work together to both prevent and respond to violence against women.

Yes, Australia needs to vastly improve its response to violence and trauma to prevent further violence. But if we are serious about preventing violence before it starts, we also need primary prevention to educate young people on how to respond to emerging challenges online, and to ensure schools, universities, workplaces and sporting clubs are safer for women. And we need to stay focused on what the evidence tells us works.

Losing It suggests that *Change the Story*, Australia's national framework for primary prevention, is based on untested theories rather than the best available evidence. This is demonstrably untrue. *Change the Story* was developed through two years of rigorous consultation and review, not in an isolated office but in a process that involved victim-survivors, frontline services, governments and leading prevention academics all over the country. It is grounded in decades of Australian and international research, was reviewed again in 2021 and updated based on over 500 pieces of new evidence. It is one of the most thoroughly examined and evidence-based frameworks in the world for preventing violence against women – and it has been put into action by organisations, practitioners, educators and governments across the country.

Gender equality work is part of the DNA of Australia's collective response to preventing violence against women – and it goes beyond the approach of any single group. Our Watch works alongside frontline services, educators, researchers, governments and countless community organisations – including the Office for Women, the Australian Human Rights Commission, the Workplace Gender Equality Agency, the national code for universities to reduce sexual assault, and many others who share this mission.

Losing It also incorrectly suggests that Our Watch has ignored alcohol, gambling, childhood trauma and other factors that contribute to violence. Again, this is demonstrably false. Both editions of *Change the Story* explicitly call for action to regulate alcohol and gambling, address harmful drinking cultures and support healing from trauma. For example, it calls for:

- stronger regulation of alcohol to challenge social norms that link drinking and violence
- targeted work to challenge male-dominated drinking cultures
- support for early intervention, healing, and trauma-informed responses
- addressing gambling and other social stressors that can intensify violence.

At the same time, gender inequality remains at the centre, because the overwhelming weight of global evidence confirms it as the most consistent driver of violence against women at a population level. This is not just Our Watch's view – it is the position of countless other organisations, including the United Nations, the World Health Organization and the Australian Human Rights Commission.

While Hill describes a range of well-documented problems, her essay lacks any nuanced discussion of the kinds of intersectional solutions needed to address the experiences of women who face the combined impacts of gender inequality and other forms of discrimination. *Change the Story*, on the other hand, calls for action on the numerous intersecting forms of oppression that influence the dynamics of violence, including colonialism, racism and ableism. Taking an intersectional approach to preventing violence is a cornerstone of primary prevention work.

We are already seeing real shifts, but primary prevention is still emerging – many areas of the country have barely started this work. It needs scale and time to have the national impact we all want. No major social change – whether it's smoking, seatbelt use or drink-driving – happens overnight. We didn't stop advocating for these reforms because change was hard, and we can't stop now when women's lives are at stake.

Hill's work points to areas where more action is needed – and we agree. More action is urgently needed to address the problems of alcohol, gambling and childhood trauma, all of which help perpetuate the devastating cycle of violence against women. But this is not an either/or choice. Women, children and young people experiencing violence need every part of the system working together – prevention, trauma-informed early intervention, frontline services, healing and recovery. As Australia's Domestic and Family Violence Commissioner, Micaela Cronin, has said, we need unity and coordination across the whole sector.

We know this work is hard – and that it takes constant learning and adaptation. Through history, every significant social change has faced backlash. But that has never been a reason to stop fighting for what's right.

Patty Kinnersly

LOSING IT

Correspondence

Helen Keleher

Jess Hill's *Losing It* presents a powerful call to action on the crisis of violence against women and children. However, her framing of prevention misrepresents both the evidence that underpins prevention and the work being done on the ground. In doing so, she undermines the dedicated efforts of a highly skilled but under-recognised, feminised workforce whose contributions are crucial to shifting the social conditions that enable gendered violence.

While her analysis begins from legitimate outrage over the continuing murders of women, it redirects that anger towards those working to advance gender equality and implement evidence-based prevention strategies, the national framework *Change the Story* and the role of Our Watch. This mischaracterisation undermines the significant progress that feminist-informed primary prevention has made in shifting patriarchal cultural norms and institutional practices.

Contrary to Hill's implication that Our Watch controls prevention, funding for primary prevention comes from a wide range of sources, including all levels of government, business, unions, banks and other corporations. Response funding comes primarily from governments.

In *Losing It*, Hill sets up a divisive "us versus them" confection that pits response work against prevention. To imply that funding one always comes at the expense of the other is misleading and divisive. Response agencies are underfunded and overstretched but have a dedicated workforce who are experts in providing front-line support to victim-survivors and agencies. Prevention expertise lies not in crisis response, but in shifting the social norms, structures and conditions that enable violence. Prevention practitioners are highly skilled, experienced and collaborative, working across systems, engaging communities, building partnerships and collaborating to constantly learn and strengthen their approaches.

Hill's critique lands heavily on workforces who are operating under significant strain, and who are overwhelmingly feminised and underpaid. Hill's framing risks invalidating their knowledge and expertise, suggesting that their work is ineffective, without engaging with its complexity, scale or the progress already made. They don't have the time or platforms to respond to sweeping public critiques – nor do they have access to the media or publishing avenues that more prominent commentators can leverage. Even so, *Losing It* consistently fails to engage with any counterarguments that have been provided in response to her ongoing campaign against prevention work. Hill fails to acknowledge that without primary prevention, demand for response services will never end.

Hill also sets up an unnecessary opposition between psychology and prevention, each of which use different tools and frameworks designed for different purposes. Primary prevention works at a population level to get the reach and cultural shifts that individual psychological treatment, such as men's behaviour change, cannot affect. Despite Hill's assertion to the contrary, *Change the Story* explicitly recognises men's behaviour change as a critical component within the larger, integrated body of prevention work, rather than as one approach competing with others. And men's behaviour change programs recognise that an understanding of the broad social context that enables violence is necessary for working with men to change their behaviour.

Preventing gender-based violence is not simply about raising awareness or providing education in isolation. It involves structural change, including equal pay, gender-equitable workplaces, universal childcare, legal protections, and cultural shifts in how we understand power and gender. Much of this work is invisible, long-term and intergenerational. It is designed for sustainable change, not to produce immediate headlines. We do have evidence that prevention practice is working, but both the backlash against gender equity and the valorisation of harmful expressions of masculinity are being sanctioned across the globe. As Hill puts it, a brazen misogyny is on the march. Indeed, the drivers described in *Change the Story* are universal. They also explain the causes of escalating rates of violence, which drinking and gambling, as exacerbating risk factors, do not. Open and honest debate, as Hill calls for on these factors or other prevention approaches, is not how knowledge is advanced, because debate is often loaded with ideology rather than the best evidence available, or with the noisiest and sometimes least informed voices.

Hill's essay uses a recurring straw-man fallacy to position feminism as an obstacle to the prevention of violence against women. Despite what Hill claims, *Change the Story* has never made the claim that it would "end the war" waged against women by men once and for all, nor is it about handing victory to "feminists," as if there is some kind of competition with psychologists. What is the war? A gender war? A political war?

A further straw man is the conflation of online feminist commentary, often informal or polemical, with the structured, evidence-based work of primary prevention practitioners and gender equity initiatives. This blurring is misleading and harmful, as it misrepresents the rigour, scope and intent of Australia's national prevention efforts.

To diminish or dismiss this workforce – and the discipline of primary prevention itself – is to misunderstand how public health works. Just as we don't judge the effectiveness of anti-smoking campaigns by looking at individual smokers in isolation, we can't assess prevention by cherry-picking anecdotes or demanding instant results. Prevention practitioners deserve recognition, investment and trust, not scapegoating or rhetorical sidelining.

Hill consistently merges calls for new approaches to prevention with victim-survivor stories to support her assertion that prevention is not working, but we know prevention is working because there is evidence of change. National surveys show a gradual but significant shift in community attitudes towards gender equality, with increasing numbers of Australians rejecting victim-blaming narratives and supporting gender equity in relationships. Change is happening through legislation that now requires organisations to ensure their staff are safe; young people are learning about respect and consent; sexist stereotypes are constantly challenged; and much more. Prevention is working when we see the ripple effects through society, which (mostly) no longer excuses men's violence, or sees sexism as just a joke, and when there is widespread outrage when women are murdered because of their gender.

There is, finally, a widespread movement that shares knowledge about how to reduce rates of violence and stop the violence before it occurs. Many, many government departments in our states and territories and non-government national and state-based organisations are involved in developing, implementing and evaluating prevention programs. No single organisation is pulling any strings on prevention approaches. It is manufactured outrage for Hill to maintain a rage against Our Watch as if prevention work begins and ends with it.

Hill's critique oversimplifies a complex system and inadvertently undermines those working within prevention frameworks who are equally committed to ending violence. The truth is we need it all: prevention, early intervention, response and recovery, working systematically. Pitting these systems against each other feeds into a political ideology that denounces women's rights to live free from violence. Our challenge is not choosing between feminism and psychology or between frontline support and cultural change, but resourcing a holistic, evidence-based system that honours the expertise of all involved. There are no quick solutions, but prevention is working, and it is essential.

Helen Keleher

This response was written with the assistance of Jackson Fairchild and Kit McMahon.

Correspondence

Anne Summers

"Policymakers can make a choice: either they can acknowledge and act on what the evidence is telling us and get curious about why gender-based violence (especially sexual violence) is increasing among young people, or they can stick their fingers in their ears and carry on doing the same old thing," journalist and author Jess Hill wrote on LinkedIn in early April, shortly after the publication of her Quarterly Essay.

She, and others, have documented the precipitous drop in income that too often follows leaving a violent relationship, with families forced to subsist on poverty-level government payments if their youngest child is aged over fourteen. We are only too familiar with ex-partners who "game" the child-support payment system and evade both payment and penalty. Increasingly, children are being acknowledged as victims in their own right, not just damaged appendages of their traumatised mothers. Their lives, too, are shattered, and without immediate support they are at risk of transmitting their trauma to the next generation.

If we want to prevent violence, especially murders, we better start helping the many men and boys whose witnessing of parental violence, including stabbings and suicide and, among immigrants and refugees, the brutalities of war, make them prime candidates for delivering violence later in their lives.

But there are no services. Teenage boys are not welcome in most shelters. Their desperate mothers are often called upon to make a "Sophie's choice" – to save herself and her other children and let her son take his chances in the youth refuge system, to scrounge on the streets or surrender to the child protection / youth detention system where the young man is likely to end up (in New South Wales at least) living, alone, in a motel guarded by state-appointed custodians. Hill cites the cost of such care: $400,000 to remove a child and $3320 per day to jail them. Counselling not included.

Where do you think the next generation of abusers is coming from? And why are they getting younger and younger? Especially the sexual abusers?

Hill's credibility is underscored by the fact she does not represent any sector or institution. Her background as a journalist equips her to gather large amounts of information and use this to deliver the kinds of critical judgements that are often not possible for those with a stake in the system. (Hill was recently appointed an industry professor at the Business School at UTS, where I am also located and, like her, funded by philanthropy. These appointments are outside the traditional academic system; they are for a fixed term, not part of the academic career structure and do not involve teaching.)

As the opening pages of Hill's essay reveal, she is well informed on the details of the horrendous violence too many women and children in this country are subjected to at the hands of men who supposedly love them. Despite this, she appears to retain an optimism that seemingly belies the title of her essay. All is not lost, she concludes. "No country in the world has cracked the problem of violence against women and children," are her concluding words to this essay. "With courage, Australia could be the first."

These words conclude a lengthy and mostly pessimistic analysis of the many ways in which Australia's policies to reduce or prevent this violence are ill-conceived, contradictory and even counterproductive. It is no wonder violence is increasing, Hill argues, when its known causes are disregarded or actually reinforced, when proven preventative measures are ignored, and governments rely on faulty theories of change.

When facing a monstrosity of the scale and malevolence of domestic, family and sexual violence, it makes no sense to adopt a David versus Goliath strategy, which the federal government seems to have done (although they would never see it that way). This strategy is one the late historian Barbara Tuchman would have described as a folly. Her legendary phrase described history as "the march of folly." While Tuchman focused on military battles, I think her method is nevertheless instructive for where we find ourselves today in trying to defeat domestic violence. A folly, Tuchman says, is a "pursuit of policy contrary to self-interest." Like locking up teenage boys so they will grow into embittered young men intent on taking revenge for what was done to them, while we pretend to be working to reduce rates of violence. Tuchman's most famous example is the Trojan horse the Greek army inveigled the city of Troy into allowing through its protective city gates. Therein lay a different approach to war, one that we might learn some lessons from.

There are many causes of violence and if most of them could be tackled at more or less the same time, our rates of violence would tumble. But it means doing a lot of things governments have yet to find the spine to pursue. Just some examples:

restrict the sale of alcohol, especially late-night home deliveries; restrict the advertising of alcohol and gambling during sporting events; ban online gambling.

In 2024 the National Cabinet formed the Rapid Review of Prevention Approaches, to provide urgent advice on how to respond to the "national emergency" of a spate of women's deaths. Jess and I were on the six-member panel which reported to the federal government in August that year. Not much has been heard since of our recommendations but they are worth pursuing because they involve precisely that mix of policies and approaches essential to implement if the government is ever to achieve its ambitious pledge *to end all domestic, family and sexual violence in a single generation*. Let's open that Trojan horse and collect our ammunition.

As stated above, Australia has an official policy to end – not reduce, *end* – all domestic, family and sexual violence "within a single generation." This pledge was made by the Minister for Social Services, Senator Amanda Rishworth, in November 2022, when she released *The National Plan to End Violence Against Women and Children 2022–2032*, a document that all jurisdictions signed off on. Known as the Second National Plan, it replaced the first such plan, which ran from 2010 to 2022 and which undertook to *reduce* violence against women and their children. The first plan failed miserably in this goal, with rates of violence, including murder, increasing during its life. A lack of targets, as well as any measures for achieving them, was blamed for this catastrophic outcome.

The first draft of the Second Plan also contained no targets but after an uproar from prominent feminists, changes were made and clear targets were included, as well as the extraordinary pledge to end all domestic violence by 2047 (assuming a generation is twenty-five years). Mostly, these targets entailed improving community attitudes, on the theory that violence would be reduced if people could be persuaded this was a worthwhile and necessary goal. They also included two astonishingly ambitious physical targets: to lower the rate of women killed by an intimate partner by 25 per cent per year, and to halve *all* forms of violence and abuse towards Aboriginal and Torres Strait Islander women and children by 2031.

There is simply no chance that these targets can or will be achieved. In the very first year of operation of the Second Plan, domestic homicides spiked by 28 per cent.

Hill devotes considerable attention to her major criticism of both plans: their reliance on the strategy document that guides them both. *Change the Story* was released in 2015 and is based on the theory that changing community attitudes to violence, relaxing rigid gender norms, giving women greater independence and teaching young people how to have respectful relationships will end violence. She, and many others, fault *Change the Story* for its reliance on gender inequality as a primary cause of violence. This not only ignores the evidence from the Nordic countries, which have the world's highest rates of gender equality but even higher rates of domestic violence, it also discounts the contribution of proven risk factors such as substance abuse, childhood maltreatment and cultures of parental dominance. *Change the Story*, writes Hill "explicitly advised governments to elevate 'primary prevention' – which targets the whole population – above and beyond other forms of prevention that work with at-risk groups."

Telling all men they are potential wife-beaters or rapists has not turned out to be a very productive strategy. It means they don't take the overall message seriously (since it's not them, so why bother) or they feel resentful and perhaps develop feelings of hostility that had previously lain dormant. Nor has ignoring the radicalisation of young men that has been taking place online for the past decade or more, introducing younger and younger kids, especially boys, to porn images that have guided their views of what sex is – and should be. While the sexual abuse of children has, thankfully, declined markedly, little kids are picking up the slack. Hill records that, on average, six Victorian incidents of child-on-child sexual abuse are reported weekly to police. Some of these are from childcare centres! We are growing our domestic, family and sexual crime rate at a rapid rate, and if we don't take drastic, multi-sector and comprehensive preventive action immediately, we will be totally unable to deal with what is coming.

Picking up her quote from the beginning of this essay, Hill goes on to state: "In which case, they may as well prepare their 2035 media statements now, apologising again for having failed to reduce gender-based violence." She wrote this before the third week of the federal election, when five women died from male violence, four of them from domestic violence, several of them in the most horrifyingly brutal circumstances imaginable. Yet at the time of writing, none of the major parties has even mentioned domestic violence, let among femicide, on the campaign trail. That has been left to the teals (all of whom are women).

It is quite incomprehensible that the governments of Australia came together less than a year ago to ask for a rapid review of prevention measures, one that would tell them what they could do to prevent this violent onslaught that has marred our country.

They won't be able to say they weren't warned.

Anne Summers

Correspondence

Marcia Neave

Describing a cultural or social problem as "wicked" means that its causes are complex and hotly debated, that it requires responses from many different systems, and that it lacks clear solutions. Jess Hill's illuminating essay illustrates why violence against women and children should be treated as a wicked problem, when considering how to prevent, or at least substantially reduce, it. As H.L. Mencken cynically observed, "For every complex problem there is an answer that is clear, simple and wrong." So it is for violence against women and children. Hill describes the recent Australian history of attempts to stop violence against women and children and how these attempts have often been influenced by the oversimplified view that social and economic gender inequality is the main cause of violence against women.

The *National Plan to Reduce Violence against Women and their Children* 2010–2022 sought to bring together Australian, state and territory government actions to achieve a "significant and sustained reduction in violence against women and their children." The plan aimed to raise community awareness of gendered violence, improve the position of women in public life, and teach boys and girls to abandon gender stereotypes and build respectful relationships. This emphasis on preventing family violence by addressing gender inequality was continued in 2015 with the release of *Change the Story*, the strategy document produced by Our Watch. It is also apparent in The *National Plan to End Violence against Women and Children* 2022–2032, released in October 2022, although the Second National Plan gave greater recognition to the effects of family violence on children and the very high rates of violence against Aboriginal and Torres Strait Island women and children.

The focus on gender inequality is not surprising. It was not until the 1980s that feminist academics and activists began to expose the gendered nature of laws, social and legal practices and institutions. Their work revealed how patriarchal views about the proper roles of women and myths about sexual assault blinded police, prosecutors and courts to the extent and effects of domestic violence and sexual assault. Violence within families was regarded as a private matter, particularly when it occurred in middle-class families. Legal and service provision responses to it were woefully inadequate. As a young academic in the 1970s, I was sometimes invited to speak to women's groups. After those meetings, women often told me about the cruelty they and their children had endured for years and their inability to leave their partner because they feared worsening violence and social disapproval and were unable to house or support themselves and their children. Child protection systems commonly warned women their children would be removed if they did not leave violent partners, but did not give them practical support to do so. This remains a significant problem for Aboriginal women experiencing family violence, whose partners, often non-Indigenous men, may use the threat of child removal as a form of coercive control.

Changing these attitudes and systems is an important goal in preventing and responding effectively to violence against women and children. But I agree with Hill that a prevention approach which relies mainly on eradicating misogyny and increasing gender equality is likely to be "clear, simple and wrong."

The background to the terms of reference of the Victorian government's 2015 Royal Commission into Family Violence acknowledged the nature of family violence as a wicked problem, though it did not use that expression. The terms of reference covered physical and other forms of violence, including financial abuse, and were not confined to violence against women and children. They recognised that "the causes of family violence are complex and include gender inequality and community attitudes towards women. Contributing factors may include financial pressures, alcohol and drug abuse, mental illness and social and economic exclusion."

The commission's task was to recommend best-practice strategies, frameworks, policies and services to prevent family violence, ensure early intervention to protect people at risk, support victims and hold perpetrators accountable for their violence. The commission was required to consider systemic responses to violence, including reducing reoffending and changing violent and controlling behaviour, to investigate how government and community organisations could better integrate and coordinate their activities, and to provide for the evaluation and measurement of the success of the recommended strategies.

Some submissions to the commission urged it to focus mainly on addressing gender inequality, while others argued that this approach would not address the systemic and individual factors which contribute to family violence. Because its terms of reference covered all types of family violence, including violence by men and women against children, violence by children against parents and siblings, violence against people with disabilities and violence in same-sex relationships, the commission took a broad view of the causes of and appropriate responses to violence. Chapters in the report recognised the complexity of responding to the diversity of people affected by family violence, including sexual violence, either as victims or perpetrators. The report included discussion of the issues facing Aboriginal and Torres Strait Islander people; older people; people from culturally and linguistically diverse communities; people from faith communities; LGBTIQA+ people; people with disabilities; people from rural, regional and remote communities; women in prison; and women working in the sex industry.

I would argue that preventing violence requires strategies which address both violence by men against women and children, and violence against other victims. The murderous stabbings of young boys by other adolescents are recent horrendous examples. The current wave of adolescent violence against strangers has prompted community alarm and political proposals for harsher application of the criminal justice system, though research clearly shows this response is ineffective. But the need to tackle all forms of violence does not require us to ignore the unequal position of women in society as both a contributor to and a consequence of men's violence against them.

Hill refers to the ongoing dispute between the "strict adherents of the feminist model" on one side and what she calls the "psychopathology" model, which treats perpetrators' behaviour as caused by individual factors like mental illness, substance abuse and childhood trauma. She expresses the hope for "a properly negotiated peace" between disputants, commenting that there are many practitioners who occupy both sides. This is often the case in discussion of wicked problems. In Hill's words, "Two things can be true at the same time." Like her, I believe that the resolution of this dispute will help to improve prevention policy and strategy. This is consistent with the observations of forensic psychiatrist Dr Gwen Adshead in her recent BBC Reith Lectures. Adshead argues that we will only reduce violence in all its forms if we address all its risk factors and causes.

It is surprising it has taken so long to recognise the limitations of a strategy which places most of its eggs in the basket of addressing gender inequality. Three main points illustrate the problem with this approach. First, the Nordic paradox shows that even in Scandinavian countries with high levels of gender equality, violence against women continues to be a serious problem. Second, as Hill explains, statistics show associations between gendered violence and the abuse of alcohol and drugs, mental illness and gambling addiction. These links are not necessarily limited to violence against women and children, though for reasons Hill explains, family members are frequently primary targets. Third, there is limited evidence to date that programs which focus mainly on changing community attitudes to gender have had any substantial impact on the behaviour of men who kill, injure or coercively control women and children. The death toll of women killed by partners or former partners continues to rise. Research also suggests that women who suicide often have violent partners.

I am puzzled by the apparent lack of influence of the Victorian royal commission on the initial development of a national prevention strategy. Many of the commission's recommendations focused on meeting the immediate needs (including housing) of people who had already been affected by family violence and were at risk of being revictimised. But other proposals addressed factors which can help to prevent violence, including early intervention when women first seek help; changing the child protection system; addressing factors which can contribute to use of violence, including mental illness and childhood trauma; and assisting perpetrators of violence to change. The link between family violence and alcohol abuse was acknowledged in the commission's recommendation that this should be recognised in the review of Victorian liquor control legislation. Other recommendations included therapeutic responses for children who had lived in violent families and/or had used violence themselves, establishing treatment programs for young people who had been involved in sexual abuse, and developing behaviour change programs for adolescents. There were also recommendations designed to improve data collection and ensure program evaluation.

Although it has taken time for some of these issues to be reflected in the national strategies intended to prevent violence against women and children, I acknowledge that a more nuanced approach is now gaining ground. The recommendations of the Rapid Review of Prevention Approaches were released in August 2024, and the review placed more emphasis than earlier plans on protecting women and children by treating every point of contact for women, including the health system, other types of service provision and the justice system, as sources of immediate support and intervention. It made recommendations about identifying high-risk perpetrators, reducing their risk of reoffending and, where possible, changing perpetrator behaviour. It recommended further funding for men's behaviour change programs, including provision of more resources to help violent men deal with substance abuse, histories of trauma and mental ill-health. It recognised the importance of helping children who had been affected by violence to recover from trauma and life disruption, which may lead them to use violence themselves.

The rapid review also proposed that governments review and tighten the regulation of alcohol supply, advertising and delivery timeframes, place a total ban on gambling advertising, and examine the relationship between the density of electronic gaming machines, online gambling and violence. At a state level these proposals are likely to be politically controversial and difficult to achieve, despite their importance.

The review's report refers to the changing role of technology, which can provide opportunities for educating individuals and the community about responding to violence against women and children but can also contribute to or exacerbate it. High-profile influencers can negatively affect boys' views about masculinity. Their influence on social media, as well as pornography, may induce men to try out violent and dangerous sexual activities such as strangulation, and persuade young women to regard this as normal sexual behaviour. The recently announced ban on children under sixteen accessing social media symbolically recognises these dangers, though it remains to be seen whether mechanisms to verify the age of users will work.

I agree with Hill that attitudinal change, standing alone, is insufficient to prevent use of violence, unless we also focus on helping men and boys to change violent behaviour. Accepting the complexity of violence against women and children is a step towards more effective approaches to prevention and response. Collecting reliable data is vital to determine the effects of the proposals discussed above and whether they also reduce violence in other contexts. I hope that in the future prevention strategies will also consider how to reduce the numbers of men and boys who are killed or victimised, or whose lives are ruined by their own use of violence.

During the period that I have worked on this issue, there have been improvements in justice and other responses to violence against women and children. But we do not yet fully understand why people inflict physical and other forms of violence on their partners and children, whom they profess to love, and on strangers. The main hope for change lies in experimenting with new approaches, collecting data and evaluating the evidence about what works and what approaches should be abandoned because they are ineffective. As the rapid review recommends, this evaluative function could be undertaken by the National Domestic, Family and Sexual Violence Commission.

Marcia Neave

Correspondence

Michael Salter

Jess Hill's essay is a klaxon call for accountability – not only for the men who perpetrate violence, or those who enable it, but for the publicly funded prevention organisations and professionals tasked with protecting the community. Drawing on her deep scholarship and advocacy, Jess highlights the dangerous simplicity imposed by the current Australian primary prevention framework, contrasting it with the true complexity of gender-based violence.

Primary prevention, by nature, demands that we focus our attention on specific opportunities for change. However, on contentious issues like violence against women and children, policymaking can become confined by political and ideological boundaries. As child protection scholar Beatrix Campbell once aptly noted, "Seeing is believing, we're told, and yet evidence, like beauty, is in the eye of the beholder." Jess points to the evidence that has been systematically sidelined in the national mission to end violence – including data many find deeply uncomfortable.

In my own work as a child abuse researcher, I've seen how reluctant we are to confront data showing that abused children, without adequate support, are more likely to experience or perpetrate gendered violence later in life. At a 2014 consultation session for the development of the national prevention framework *Change the Story*, I raised the well-established link between child sexual abuse and adult victimisation and perpetration. The suggestion was quickly dismissed as "victim-blaming," and the conversation moved on. My point was simple: early mental health support for abused children could not only improve their wellbeing but also protect them and future generations from violence.

I had also submitted a literature review to VicHealth supporting these claims, including data on the role of trauma, poverty and alcohol abuse in shaping violent behaviours. But, as reported in *The Saturday Paper* in 2024, I was asked to remove entire sections – not because they were inaccurate, but because they didn't fit the framework's narrative. As Jess documents, the decade since has brought little progress in acknowledging or addressing these issues.

This isn't just academic frustration. When trauma, poverty and substance abuse are brushed aside in favour of a narrow pursuit of "gender equality," we leave critical drivers of violence unaddressed. As I was told during that review process, the prevention vision was of a gender-equal society, not necessarily one free from alcohol abuse or poverty. Risk factors that diverged from that path were deemed less relevant.

Following a spike in intimate partner homicides last year, Jess and I co-authored a white paper critiquing the idealism behind *Change the Story*. We called for children and child maltreatment to be placed at the centre of prevention efforts. Encouragingly, the Commonwealth government took note. Jess was appointed to a national panel on prevention, and many of our recommendations were supported at the September meeting of National Cabinet. However, backlash followed, particularly in Victoria, where the current prevention model originated and where many have built careers around promoting attitude-change-based interventions. Some of these criticisms have been personal and dismissive, rarely addressing the core issue Jess and I raised: that after a decade of unprecedented funding, violence against women and children is not falling.

When pressed, these defenders insist their approach simply needs more time or money. But this refusal to consider new evidence or adjust course reflects a greater investment in the moral certainty of gender equality (a cause that, of course, Jess and I support) than in tackling the complexity of effective prevention. Jess's essay, by contrast, honours those working outside the dominant model – those who are innovating and intervening despite the systemic blind spots of *Change the Story*.

Some critics of Jess's essay have claimed that she is raising points already acknowledged in Our Watch materials. Yet acknowledgement is not the same as implementation. In violence prevention, what matters is not what appears in a well-designed report, but what is prioritised, resourced and embedded in practice.

Jess's essay is not an attack – it is a necessary intervention. It demands that we confront the limits of our current frameworks and broaden our lens to include the full complexity of violence: its roots in childhood trauma, poverty, predatory industries like alcohol, gambling and pornography, and the political failures that allow these factors to persist. If we are serious about ending violence against women and children, we must be willing to shift not only attitudes but systems, even when doing so is uncomfortable, inconvenient or unpopular.

Michael Salter

Correspondence

Russell Marks

In *Losing It*, Jess Hill at last concludes where she might have when she first began reporting on domestic violence a decade ago: that beneath much family and domestic violence run deep currents of trauma in formative experiences. Much of the DV sector has resisted this conclusion for decades, or has at least dismissed it as irrelevant, preferring their own "woman = good, man = bad" version of carceral feminism, which consigns male "perps" to the purgatory of punishment and prison. Armed with righteous indignation and moral certainty, many researchers and practitioners in this sector have (ironically) bullied those professionals who disagree with them into cowed silence, and have ensured – as Hill now observes – that our National Plan is only about one thing: reforming backwards attitudes about gender.

Hill herself has not simply told this story; she's helped to write it. Her first essay on DV in *The Monthly*, in 2015, sang straight from the DV sector's most doctrinal hymn-sheet, which claims that men's violence against women is primarily a "choice," that power and control is the central objective, and that reforming gender attitudes is the solution. Hill wrote "Home truths" in the wake of Luke Batty's terrible, world-shattering murder by his father. Greg Anderson's violence was so brutal, so unimaginably horrific, that it shocked governments into well-overdue action. Victoria's held a royal commission. Australia's became the first in the world to commit to ending violence against women. There was a Zeitgeist. Women calling out men's violence and other bad behaviour were getting broad traction for really the first time in recorded history. Clementine Ford was at her most righteous and unrepentant, and emerged as perhaps the most identifiable figure in the new carceral feminism. The #MeToo movement ended the careers of some men with very high profiles. Out of this Zeitgeist came forthright survivor-advocates for change, including Bri Lee and, later, Grace Tame. Women were succeeding, apparently, in changing the culture.

This movement shared an objective: that violence against women was the type of violence which most urgently needed to end. This was difficult to disagree with, because women were being killed by their male partners, or male ex-partners, or sometimes their fathers or even their sons, at staggering rates. And it shared a common view of the problem: men, and their "choice" to use violence against women. Women who used violence did less damage, and hardly ever killed. Or, when they did kill, it was mostly to put an end to the relentless violence they were suffering.

But there was always a set of questions which lurked, uncomfortably unaddressed and often unasked, beneath a national conversation in which any discussion that problematised the above truths was increasingly taboo. Women were never the majority of homicide victims in any given year: most homicide victims were (and remain) men. Why, then, was domestic violence (which does overwhelmingly kill women, but accounts for "only" two in every five homicide deaths) the most urgent of all types of violence? Is it in fact useful to distinguish between types of violence at all? And is "choice" really the most useful lens, from a policy perspective, through which to see the use of violence?

For much of the last decade, Jess Hill has (as she acknowledges) been both reporter *and* advocate for ending the domestic type of violence. Maintaining both roles presumably makes it difficult, as a journalist, to critically assess other advocates. By the time she published *See What You Made Me Do* in 2019, Hill was still using the language of this movement and its researcher-advocates: men who used violence in intimate relationships, for instance, were either "pitbulls" or "cobras." Women were sympathetic victims, and when they used violence it was because they were mostly reacting to violence perpetrated on them by men. Children were sympathetic victims too, until they began to use violence themselves. And while she had begun to question the exclusive policy focus on changing gender attitudes, other factors – alcohol, drugs, mental health/illness, housing and gambling – didn't even have entries in the book's index.

Along the way, Hill became a leading voice in the movement towards the criminalisation of "coercive control," which has since been achieved across the country. Criminalisation and the carceral response in general has been the preferred approach of the DV sector, and it's one that finds favour with the state, because it shifts blame sideways (onto individual "perpetrators" of violence) rather than upwards (onto systems and agencies and policies, which are in governments' power to influence). Regrettably, what the carceral response has done – apart from sending more men to prison, where they adopt the values of a prison culture and learn even more about violence and resentment – is send more *women* to prison.

Aboriginal women are now the fastest-growing prison population in Australia. Very often they are what the movement (and now the law) calls the "true victims" of domestic violence perpetrated by men. But the definition of what constitutes "domestic violence" is now so broad that it is quite easy for men inflicting truly coercive control over women to use the legal system as an extension of their controlling behaviour. In my work as a criminal defence lawyer, I routinely see intervention orders weaponised by controlling men against what I suspect are the "true victims" of their violence. In practice, if a violent man calls police and alleges that his wife has been coercively controlling him by withholding money (so that he doesn't binge-drink or gamble), isolating him from systems of support (so that he doesn't meet his mates at the pub) and emotionally and verbally abusing him and even physically assaulting him (by occasionally "losing it" at him after she's dealt with their kids alone for days and he's come home after a bender), police are bound to take his complaint seriously. Even if she provides a statement of her own (and plenty of women in this situation don't, because they're already designated the perpetrator and are simply served with orders, or even charged), police are likely to simply make cross-orders protecting each from the other. Like most carceral responses, criminalising coercive control has been, predictably, ineffective at best. It has meant that more women have been going to prison, and it hasn't stopped women being killed by men.

In *Losing It*, Hill now asks why we've failed – and failed so abysmally that the only murder rate that's going up is that which counts the numbers of women murdered by men. After a long decade of reportage and advocacy, she concludes at last that we won't get anywhere until we begin to acknowledge the damage being done in children's formative years of abusive and neglectful parenting, and abusive and traumatic systems.

As Hill now documents, our collective failure to grasp this fundamental reality has had catastrophic consequences. Social attitudes (including about gender) take at least a generation to shift. Meanwhile, governments, sporting bodies and retailers have been free to increase their supply of alcohol and gambling practically with abandon, despite mountains of data which show correlative and even causal relationships with all kinds of violence. Child protection, youth justice, housing, education and health policies – all of which have recently enhanced their carceral drive despite decades of inquiries and recommendations for urgent reform in the opposite direction – have been siloed away from the apparently even more urgent objective of reforming gender attitudes. The result: dysregulated men *and* women continue to inflict violence, abuse and neglect on children, and too many of those children become teenagers and then adults in violent relationships. Government agencies, policies and systems continue to amplify that trauma, and pile on their own. Non-government organisations freely participate in the race for funding dollars and many end up as little more than extensions of the state – thus adding even more trauma. We now have entire systems committed to ensuring that traumatised children who behave badly know only one thing for sure: that they're bad kids who will become bad adults. Just pick up nearly any tabloid newspaper or listen to any unimaginative state or territory politician on youth crime – or, indeed, too many in the DV sector on adolescent violence.

What's wrong with all carceral responses is that instead of changing systems which foster criminal behaviour, they attempt to change individuals by punishing them. This is what much of the victims' rights movement has advocated since the 1970s, and it simply doesn't work. Indeed, we now see the carceral response everywhere: "zero tolerance" for dysregulated behaviour is now a catchphrase for our age. "Tough on the causes of crime" became a catchphrase an entire generation ago, before it was again forgotten. It is one thing to advocate for adequate support for victim-survivors of particular forms of violence. It is quite another to build policy on what victim-survivors want done to perpetrators of the violence against them.

The frustrating thing about Hill's journalism/advocacy is that all this was well known a long time ago. Like all discrete social industries that compete for scarce funding dollars, the DV sector has, regrettably, been allowed to claim that its particular focus – men's violence against women – is the most urgent problem, and has been given largely free rein to identify the causes and then propose the solutions. As a result, we've collectively confused the symptom (murder rates) with the disease. To begin to appreciate the extent to which ideology dominates the DV sector's analysis, one only needs to spend some time in organisations with other foci – such as child safety.

My field, criminal law, individualises to the point of absurdity behaviour which is, mostly, symptomatic of whatever demons grew inside a person during their childhood, and which have not since been exorcised. Delayed gratification, impulse control, appropriate control loci, emotional self-regulation, long-term thinking, an ability to distinguish one's own needs and interests from those of others, and to recognise others' need for autonomy: these are skills exhibited by well-adjusted adults, and are rarer in adults who haven't had the benefits of good-enough parenting and social support systems. Wealth doesn't guarantee those benefits. No parent wants to accept that they're inflicting harm on their children, though too many of us – including those of us with sufficient material resources – do so unwittingly. For too long, we've only been able to see the damage done to victim-survivors by the most proximate abuser. The criminal law, and the state, is comfortable with this. There are now mountains of research papers which don't look any further than the immediate perpetrator–victim relationship.

The uncomfortable reality that we've never faced is that our formative experiences are the most significant factor in whether we perpetrate violence *or* become victims of it. Often, violence is less a "choice" than an impulse. Or a compulsion. Our continued application of a moral framework (victim = sympathetic, perp = evil) obscures the fact that victims and perpetrators are often drawing from the same well of human misery – or at least adjacent wells. Some specialist DV services will even refuse to assist women victims of violence on the ground that they are also alleged to be perpetrators. This, like our entire collective response for the last decade, fundamentally misunderstands violence. Whether it is perpetrated on others, suffered at another's hands or even directed inwards at oneself (as self-harm), violence – especially in intimate relationships – is at least very often the outward expression of internal dysregulation. And traumatic experiences don't account for the whole story: whenever a child enters the turbulent waters of adolescence without enough capacity either to cope with rejection and disappointment or to recognise and avoid (rather than be attracted to, or downplay) potentially dangerous situations, there's every chance they (or those close to them) are headed for treacherous rocks.

The old set of myths about domestic violence have been replaced by new myths: that it's a special or unique kind of violence; that anyone can find themselves in an abusive relationship; that it's inexplicable except as a "choice" the perpetrator is making. But these myths make out the perpetrator to be a kind of bogeyman with terrifyingly unknowable motivations. It is certainly true that the perpetrator of violence is often terrifying. But his motivations are usually psychologically banal, his desire to exert power and control over others often explained by an upbringing that stunted his self-esteem and suppressed or denied his autonomy. And while anyone can of course become a victim of violence, whether a potential victim observes or ignores early red flags in a domestic relationship has much to do with their own psychology, itself often a legacy of formative lessons. Imagine a public conversation which asked all of us to be aware of our own roles – as parents, friends, victims *and* abusers – in the creation and perpetuation of the cycle of violence.

Advocates for survivors of violence have too often retreated into the slogans of the victims' rights movement. Any analysis which remotely resembles what it calls "victim-blaming" is now close to taboo. The unfortunate function of taboos – as Hill now recognises – is to shut down not just distasteful and disrespectful comment (which often feels like relief), but also genuine discussion of social, policy and relational solutions. For too much of the victims' rights–oriented DV sector and its researcher-advocates, ideology has proved more important than empirical reality – especially when it comes to the non-gender factors (like alcohol, gambling and mental illness) which are implicated in violence. It truly beggars belief that there are still advocates and researchers who deny that alcohol in particular is a significant cause of violent behaviour. Perhaps the most valuable feature of *Losing It* is Hill's preparedness to call out the taboos which are preventing open debate, good policy and an end to the violence.

In *Losing It*, Hill at long last points a way out of the moralising dead end of much of the DV sector's analysis, with its "perps" and "survivors" and "choices," and towards the kind of work that would need to begin if we seriously want to end the domestic type of violence. It is a much, much bigger task than the National Plan conceives, and which much of the DV sector has championed. Surely, ending domestic violence is merely part of the broader goal of ending violence in general. It requires, surely, urgent action on proximate causes and triggers (like the availability and promotion of alcohol and the push-marketing of gambling, and their association with activities like sport and socialising), an urgent commitment by governments to adequate social security and decent and affordable housing, medium-term whole-of-government work on reforming government departments, agencies and institutions away from the carceral impulse and towards an ethic of care, *and* longer-term work on changing our collective and individual attitudes to violence (which includes, but is not limited to, our ideas about gender). Hill is kind to Anthony Albanese in this election year and notes that he has recently acknowledged the National Plan's inadequacy. But at the time of writing (just before the election), neither major party has any plans to do what needs to be done. Nor does any state or territory government or Opposition. After a decade of deference to the DV sector and hollow commitments, we have not begun even to scratch the surface.

Russell Marks

LOSING IT

Correspondence

Manjula Datta O'Connor

In *Losing It*, Jess Hill continues to challenge the status quo. In my response I want to draw attention to a dimension that remains underexplored in the National Plan: how family violence is facilitated within Australia's migrant and ethnically diverse communities.

Domestic abuse is expressed, endured and silenced differently across different cultures, notwithstanding that some contributing elements such as gender inequality and mental health issues are shared. These communities are not on the margins of the national story: in 2023, 30.7 per cent of Australians were born overseas and the top ten migrant source countries include India, China, Nepal, Pakistan and Sri Lanka. We cannot overlook them. Our understanding of gendered violence has lagged in such communities. A feminist analysis of inequality is necessary but not sufficient. We need a more textured understanding – one that acknowledges the influence of tradition, family hierarchy, and migration stressors and an imbalance of power that is sometimes ferocious. Happily, we also have stories of resistance by women and men working within their communities.

In many traditional ethnic societies, the family is not just composed of the two parents and children; it is an extended network with multigenerational members, adult siblings and their partners, who share love, care and affection. And it is a system of deep support. Within this system, family wellbeing often outweighs individual concerns. Extended families provide emotional support, childcare and financial stability and help address social loneliness, often seen in single-person households. But there is a downside. If just one toxic person destabilises the system, exploiting their power, the family can become a site of unnecessary control and abuse. This can, however, be tempered by a benevolent patriarch within the family, an extended social network or a religious institution. We need to understand such nuanced factors to strengthen our communities.

Patriarchal traditions are deeply entrenched in collectivist cultures. Western cultures are patriarchal too. It is the different expressions that matter. In Indian and many other communities, sons are favoured. Elders command respect. Usually, the family is led by a male, and older women have power over younger women. Marriage is less a personal choice than a family negotiation. And within these hierarchies, marriage is the all-important thing that every woman aspires to. Single women are often positioned at the lowest rung, as are daughters-in-law – until they give birth to a child, preferably a son. The time of pregnancy and the arrival of a new baby can be joyous. But I have also heard stories about mothers-in-law dictating exactly how the baby is cared for, bathed, given or not given medicine, and more.

Then there is the problem of dowry abuse in the South Asian communities. It is an expression of gender inequality, and in turn reinforces gender inequality. The enormous power of the groom and his family over the bride and her family is open to abuse. Such power is societally endowed. That influences how a new bride who fails to bring adequate dowry will be treated. Some justify their abuse by calling insufficient dowry a show of disrespect to the groom and his family; others may attribute to it a lowering of their social status. It can become the pretext for emotional abuse, demands, coercive control, isolation from her family, exclusion within the extended family, violence, and even abandonment in Australia. I have also been contacted by some brides left behind, abandoned overseas immediately after marriage, their dowries confiscated. My research shows that about a third of the South Asian population have either experienced or known someone who has experienced dowry abuse.

Another vexed issue is that of arranged marriage. The family's control over the choice of life partner is a double-edged sword. It provides for a sensible decision made by older, wiser heads, and the final choice usually rests with the young man or woman. However, it can go terribly wrong. Some men are coerced into marrying a woman of their parents' choice – forced to give up a girlfriend, some take it out on the new bride, subjecting her to violence, confiscating the expensive dowry and abandoning her in Australia or leaving her behind in India. Finding a partner – falling in love, as in Western tradition – can be problematic too. More than half of marriages end in divorce. In the Indian culture, marrying for love may lead to violence from the extended family. I have spoken to mothers of sons in that situation who say they don't want to lose control over the choice of their daughter-in-law. These are different types of cultural contexts and require ethno-specific solutions.

Female genital cutting (FGC), forced marriage and underage marriage are manifestations of cultural practices related to societal demands for the suppression of women that are carried out by older women and men within families. They, too, require sensitive understanding and response. Often victims are silenced. Forced marriage, FGC and the dowry system subject woman to financial and emotional exploitation. For example, women from the Horn of Africa who have undergone FGC may attract higher dowries for their parents. Dowry demands by the groom's family may arise from greed: a plan to get rich quick, abandon the new wife and marry again. Additionally, violence from mothers-in-law is a significant but under-reported issue; older women may perpetuate cycles of abuse against younger daughters-in-law to assert dominance. Gender inequality drives family domestic violence against women, but societal stigma, shame and fear of criticism are significant barriers to prevention. Despite being illegal in Australia, these practices continue. There is conflict between what the law says and the pressure from the patriarchal household and society.

Migration adds yet another layer of complexity. Sponsorship of a partner contributes to power imbalance: the sponsored partner may be socially isolated and lack knowledge of the Australian legal system. An immigrant bride who is brought into the country on a temporary visa is at greater risk than one on a partner visa. She may not know her legal rights. She may not know the language. She may not even know she can leave. The Department of Home Affairs should issue a new domestic violence residency visa for sponsored victim-survivors of domestic and family violence on temporary visas, who are often wrongly identified as perpetrators. This would diminish the power of the abusive sponsor and enhance safety. Expanding eligibility and access to legal aid, housing, social security and Medicare for women on temporary visas who are experiencing domestic, family and sexual violence would prevent their return to abusive households.

For most women of the Indian subcontinent, divorce carries a stigma and can bring social exclusion. The cultural weight of shame, the pressure not to "bring dishonour" to the family and the fear of community ostracism are powerful deterrents. And the victim somehow survives silently. I have seen many victim-survivors of family violence who have endured years of abuse, coercion and control. One day, one such woman hit back in anger, with a tirade of impulsive physical anger, smashing a fence gate. Her perpetrator was able to convince the police, who often lack cultural literacy, that he was the victim and she the perpetrator. She was evicted and he gained custody of the children.

Policy responses to family violence in multicultural communities are often well-meaning, but intersectionality – understanding the additive effect of multiple disadvantages caused by the intersection of culture, migration and trauma – does not actually translate into practice. Settlement services are often reluctant to run education programs for new migrants. They may fear being seen as culturally insensitive or, worse, racist. Religious leaders, who hold immense influence, may shy away from discussing domestic violence altogether, preferring instead to uphold "family unity" at all costs.

There is no doubt that change must come from within communities. But for that to happen, institutions must offer support without judgement, legal clarity without inflexibility, and cultural understanding without compromising human rights. These are the challenges that need attention:

- **Intergenerational violence**
  Parental domestic violence is a well-known cause of intergenerational violence. A lesser-known form is a mother-in-law who once endured violence herself enforcing that same control/abuse over her daughter-in-law.

- **Economic dependency / financial abuse**
  Joint accounts and the man controlling the money is seen to signify household strength. This opens the possibility of financial control and economic abuse. Many migrant women victim-survivors of family violence do not know how their hard-earned money was spent by their husbands. Often money was sent to his family abroad. Not having access to one's own money means inability to escape. Victims have also been deceived into signing as guarantors for loans, for businesses they don't own, operate or even know about. Some were made directors of companies they knew nothing about, only to be left with a huge debt after separation.

- **Cultural and religious norms**
  Traditional gender norms are sometimes not recognised as injustice but seen as duty. Religious interpretations can be used to sanctify submission. Resistance, then, is not only social but spiritual too.

- **Community backlash**
  Women who speak out, leave their marriage or seek help can face rejection from their biological families. Social exclusion of separated women is traumatising in tightly knit communities; the fear of "bringing shame" reinforces silence. The victims remain trapped and learn to suffer silently.

- **Legal illiteracy**
  Many women do not know that practices like dowry abuse, FGC or forced marriage are illegal. Some frontline responders do not know either – or hesitate to act in culturally complex situations.

The solutions are not abstract. They are already in motion, often at the grassroots level:

- **Engaging faith leaders**
  When religious leaders speak against family violence, change is possible. The government funds support programs for leaders, training and resources. Sermons that denounce violence can be powerful.

- **Adapting parental education programs**
  Programs like Triple P Parenting must be retooled to reflect cultural realities. Delivery in language, through ethno-specific facilitators, is essential. Mothers-in-law should be included as well as mothers and fathers.

- **Legal literacy and outreach**
  Workshops tailored to new migrants, in community settings, can be a useful settlement tool. Migrants get to compare their own laws and traditions with the prevailing mainstream Australian practices – for example, in childrearing. Thus, they demystify Australian laws and gender etiquette. The AustralAsian Centre for Human Rights and Health, among others, has materials ready, but funding is perennially scarce.

- **Media as mirror and catalyst**
  Social media, television and storytelling must reflect the lived realities of diverse communities. My organisation has created documentaries and campaigns that do just this, explaining how toxic gender norms are built and how they can be unbuilt.

- **Men as allies**
  Not all sons are pampered. Some are partners in change. Positive male role models, fatherhood programs and workplace gender policies all help reshape the next generation.

To close, I note that the other side of the intersectional coin – the experience of immigrant men – has remained comparatively underexplored. How do mental health conditions, shaped by stigma, cultural expectations and limited access to care, contribute to the perpetration of violence in these communities? This is not a call for sympathy towards perpetrators. It is a call for clarity. If we are to reduce the rates of family and domestic violence, we must look unflinchingly at all contributing factors. Mental health is one of them. That means rethinking how we design perpetrator intervention programs. It means integrating mental health support, not as an excuse but as a method of accountability. If someone is depressed, anxious or suffering from a personality disorder, we cannot allow that to become a shield from justice. But nor can we afford to ignore it, because untreated illness increases the likelihood of repeated harm.

Manjula Datta O'Connor

Correspondence

Marilyn Beaumont

In *Losing It*, Jess Hill critiques Australia's approach to the primary prevention of violence against women and children. She says, "somewhere along the way, however, this hypothesis hardened into something more like doctrine. But evidence is not static – it must be constantly evaluated and updated." Her essay presents a limited perspective, with inaccuracies and no understanding of the process and layering of primary prevention.

I have over forty years' experience in health services, policy development, management, health promotion and advocacy. My understanding and witnessing the impact of domestic violence comes from a health practitioner's perspective and a personal perspective. Working as a nurse for many years, I have provided individual care; I have also led large-scale primary prevention focused on the whole population.

I do not support an approach to ending violence before it occurs that is based on personal history (psychopathology) – or (as Jess describes it) "aberrant" or "'sick' individuals [who] … harm people they claim to love" – because this longstanding complex social problem cannot be solved by treating a few "bad" people. To solve such a complex problem there must be resources at the top of the cliff – primary prevention – so people don't fall off, *and* ambulances – tertiary prevention – to deal with the injured at the bottom of the cliff! Both are essential, always.

Men's violence against women (while not all family or domestic violence is perpetrated by men against women, the majority is) is complex. It arises from deeply held, often highly emotional beliefs, value systems, stereotypes and power relationships. The attitudes and behaviours that support it are mostly invisible and taken for granted. There is a demonstrated strong link between violence against women and systemic inequalities rooted in structural power imbalances between men and women. Justifications for violence that focus primarily on individual behaviour and psychopathology, such as alcohol abuse or a history of exposure to violence, overlook the broader impact of systemic gender inequality and women's subordination. Any change at the individual aberrant behaviour end won't stick, won't be sustained, without change to the systemic inequalities.

Australia's primary prevention of violence against women is informed by a public health model. This approach strives to address the social, political and economic determinants of health to achieve a complete state of physical, mental and social wellbeing for individuals and communities, and to empower people to take charge of their own health. Using this approach, primary prevention programs focus on promoting equal and respectful relationships and on changing the cultures, norms, policies and laws that support or condone violence and disrespect.

The project of preventing gender-based violence is long-term, challenging and constantly evolving, as the evidence develops and our social contexts change. It includes working across legislation, public policy, funding, education, research, developing workforce capacity, advocacy, openness and accountability, informed and active consumers, with continuous quality improvement and continual vigilance to keep moving forward. This is vastly different to the way that Jess writes in her essay about advertising as a campaign and Australia's approach to the prevention of domestic violence as static. In this she is wrong.

Primary prevention of violence against women requires constant vigilance and scanning of the external environment; to know and understand risks and opportunities to take the work further; to research, pilot and evaluate interventions, creating evidence where it is absent; to translate this evidence into action and practice; and to develop and maintain an authorising and enabling environment within which to keep moving forward.

An example of evidence-building that leads practice comes from my time as CEO of Women's Health Victoria. In 2001 we wrote that epidemiological data of presenting conditions and hospital admissions didn't measure the extent and impact of violence against women. What was being counted was the presenting condition, such as fractures or broken bones sustained by violent acts. It was critical to connect the health problems arising *from* the experience of violence *with* the experience of violence. Our paper contributed to a 2004 VicHealth study, 'The Health Costs of Violence: Measuring the Burden of Disease Caused by Intimate Partner Violence', which then informed an Access Economics report on the financial costs of intimate partner violence: for one year, $8.1 billion. This work clearly demonstrated that violence was prevalent, serious, preventable and costly.

The health impact of violence against women and children wasn't new. What was new was the translation of this new evidence into policy and practice across a wide range of jurisdictions. Work to translate evidence into practice in new ways, particularly across primary prevention, has been continuing in many jurisdictions and settings. Jess only refers to schools and sport.

To prepare for new action in line with the newly compiled evidence, the discourse about violence against women had to shift away from it being a *shameful, secret, private matter* to the view that it is a crime. This involved changing community norms and attitudes and teaching agencies, institutions and individuals to understand the root causes of violence against women. While I think we have come a long way, this work is never done, never complete.

I know of many jurisdictions and settings where primary prevention action is being taken and is continuing to build the evidence base. Women's Health Victoria's Take a Stand Against Domestic Violence program underpins the Australian Football League's Respect and Responsibility program.

There are health settings, including in women's, babies' and children's health, where care is changing with the introduction of sensitive practice and competence in identifying domestic violence, in all its forms – developing the capacity to intervene early and foster equal and respectful parenting relationships. This has mobilised health workers to be active in their workplaces, their communities and their own lives. This, too, is primary prevention, early intervention and response.

Jess describes a "fifty-year-old turf war." "We're flanked by two armies: strict adherents to the 'feminist' model on one side, and loyalists of the 'psychopathology' model on the other."

I have not been in a fifty-year turf war, nor has my advocacy been about a strict adherence to a feminist model. The World Health Organization states that "violence against women – particularly intimate partner violence and sexual violence – is a major public and clinical health problem and a violation of women's human rights. It is rooted in and perpetuates gender inequalities." Prevention, early intervention and response to violence against women must go hand in hand. Prevention is a traditionally underfunded area. It is imperative that these three areas are not competing for a limited funding pool.

I am a feminist and nurse who has been involved in a lifetime of advocacy using a world-accepted framework, creating evidence and translating this into practice, and mainstreaming what we have learnt. We have come far, and in this I stand proud.

Marilyn Beaumont

Correspondence

Anne Manne

Whatever works. That has to be the simple benchmark for assessing the effectiveness of the nation's response to violence against women and children. After more than a decade, with millions of government dollars spent and several national action plans, the problem is getting worse, not better. Women are being murdered at *increasing* rates, while sexual violence is ever crueller and inflicted by ever younger men. Chillingly, Jess Hill establishes that lower death rates have not been due to less deadly violence. Rather, it is the improved speed of ambulance responses that saves lives.

Why? What has gone so badly wrong?

It is into this fraught and highly contested territory that Jess Hill steps with her exemplary Quarterly Essay. Hill provides both a sharp analysis of what's wrong but also a radical intervention reframing the issue. Hill is an invaluable guide. Her groundbreaking 2019 book *See What You Made Me Do* provided many women with the language and concepts to understand their experience – including coercive control and gaslighting – for the first time. Like that book, this Quarterly Essay has an impressive scope and grasp of the evidence.

Hill's essay is also courageous. Groupthink – safe conformity, even obedience to the dominant paradigm – is rarely helpful in bending the arc towards justice. While enduring sleepless nights while undergoing chemotherapy for brain cancer, Hill decided to step away from a prevailing groupthink; the "doctrinal rigidity" over the "ameliorative" or "primary prevention" approach, whereby changing "drivers" like sexism, and achieving gender equality, will eventually make domestic violence disappear. Well-meaning, worthy, but rather next-century. The plan was clearly not working. Domestic violence remains as destructive and intractable a problem as it ever was, and sexual violence against women is getting worse.

Hence Hill, in *Losing It*, suggests that our too-exclusive focus on the gender equity strategy at the expense of other potential areas of intervention is problematic. We need to pivot to another strategy. The ideological trenches in this area have been aggressively patrolled. Despite the nasty fallout and personal attacks on Jess Hill (and Michael Salter), their integrity, good sense and purity of motive have been both steadfast and admirable.

It is important to understand that Hill is not arguing for an "either/or" approach when it comes to strategies to prevent domestic violence. Although she *supports* the gender equity paradigm, her critique is of an exclusive focus to the exclusion of other more immediate causes and solutions – alcohol and drug abuse, gambling, pornography, boys turning to the toxic phlegm of a misogynist manosphere, children suffering from intergenerational trauma, men whose inner life is messed up by trauma and consequent severe attachment disorders. It was eye-opening and disturbing to realise that education on gender equality has either made little headway or even created a backlash among young males, who look to Andrew Tate to shore up a narcissistic sense of superiority. Insecure, traumatised males struggling with shame, whose inner lives are so messed up, are especially easy pickings for those promulgating a grandiose male supremacist narrative.

It was equally disturbing to read Hill's account of the "Nordic paradox," whereby those nations most advanced in achieving gender equality actually have *higher* rates of domestic violence than more patriarchal societies. One depressing possibility is that women are more likely to be punished as they move *away* from a traditional, unthreatening and subservient role. Likewise, an astonishing amount of the Trump counter-revolution is about re-establishing conservative gender norms, including the suggestion of bestowing a Motherhood Medal on women who have six or more children. (Just as the Nazis did.)

Hill highlights the importance of the perpetrator's inner life, particularly the role of shame. Coercive control is a huge element in intimate partner violence. But *why* are these men so controlling? Trauma leads not only to insecure attachments in children, but also to the most problematic, disorganised and disorientated attachments. Abuse and trauma can lead to a shamed identity. One antidote to shame is a male grandiosity, dominating and coercively controlling a woman who is expected to service all of his needs, what he wants and when he wants it. It is a subtype of pathological narcissism which mainlines misogyny. To put it another way, patriarchy creates narcissistic men.

A narcissist in the grip of humiliated fury – when challenged or when their partner wants to leave – is *dangerous*. One common shame response is to enter "ATTACK OTHER" script; to lower, even destroy, the other person. Analysing how perpetrators might be dealing with unbearable levels of shame needs, however, to be carefully handled lest it offer an exonerating narrative for someone who has committed a heinous murder.

Hill points to Natalie Siegel-Brown's work, based on "good strong bloody neuroscience" linking trauma to violence. "Where does his need for power and control come from?" Hill asks. "It can't only be entitlement … men go to such extremes they end up ruining their own lives." Australia has high levels of child maltreatment. Given the link between trauma and later intimate partner violence, we need a trauma-informed approach and intervention when the damage is done, in childhood and adolescence. The link between trauma and violence is clear. A traumatised boy grows into "an adult who is constantly seeking power and control over their environment. They develop an insatiable appetite for it … including coercive control and sexual violence." Given the robust social science evidence which exists on childhood trauma, damage to attachment and problematic life trajectories, it is hard to understand why it has been ignored. Intervention *has* to be in childhood.

A strength of the essay is Hill's emphasis on children. They have for too long been treated as collateral damage. Although they are victim-survivors in their own right, all the emphasis has been on the adult victim-survivor. Children fleeing violent circumstances are receiving little help. Hill gives a heartbreaking account of the Care Hotels, where abused, traumatised and homeless children are kept in detention for extended periods of time. Their caregivers are a constantly rotating set of strange faces, present so fleetingly that it is impossible to form crucial alternative attachment bonds. These children are truly in limbo. Yet it costs a fortune. Why are we willing to pay for such damaging out-of-home care, but so miserly in our support for families on the brink, long before separation becomes necessary?

In such a richly researched piece, it seems churlish to mention some lacunae. Hill mentions but does not discuss at length misogynistic and increasingly violent pornography as a risk factor. It is as addictive as gambling and alcohol and is now omnipresent in young people's lives at ever earlier ages. Hill presents alarming evidence that victims are getting younger and the sexual violence more severe. She quotes Di Macleod, who has led the Gold Coast Centre Against Sexual Violence for thirty-five years. "Anal rape and strangulation especially are everyday experiences for women reporting to our service," she says. "Back in 1990, I can probably think of about four people who reported that." What's the difference now? Porn.

Marie Crabbe's important work with young people and secondary-school kids shows the problematic effect of easily available and widespread porn use on young men's sexual behaviour. In particular, Crabbe points to terrible risks from the normalisation of strangulation as a common sexual practice. Crabbe's initiative "It's Time We Talked" is a prevention program about porn and harmful sexual behaviours. Far more needs to be done in this space, given how violent misogynistic porn is influencing the next generation of perpetrators.

Although Hill emphasises alcohol abuse, I think drug abuse is surely as important, especially for younger people. Drugs like ice also act to radically disinhibit aggression.

In many of the cases I read about, there is lack of action by police, often based on ignorance of intimate partner violence and appalling bias against women, despite clear evidence of imminent or actual harm. Too often we see inaction due to the distorted thinking behind remarks like that of Detective Inspector Mark Thompson about Hannah Clarke and her children, burned to death by Rowan Baxter, that it could be a case of a "husband driven too far." It was a revealing snapshot of problematic attitudes among police.

When this was penned, twenty-five women had already been killed this year. This femicide is a national emergency, surely. Yet during the 2025 election campaign there was a deafening silence on domestic violence until weeks into the campaign, and then the response of both major parties was vague. Time to pivot!

Anne Manne

LOSING IT

Correspondence

Bob Pease

As an activist and scholar in the violence prevention field for over forty years, I have often been critical of government approaches to address men's violence against women, including that of the National Plan and Our Watch's *Change the Story*. However, my criticism is not that they are too feminist or gender-biased; rather it is that they are not feminist enough.

Jess Hill's commitment and passionate engagement with the issue of violence against women is widely acknowledged and appropriately acclaimed. She has that important journalistic skill of using the written word to convey the outrage that so many people feel about the increasing levels of violence. Her earlier co-authored paper with Michael Salter, *Rethinking Primary Prevention*, resonated with many while receiving pushback from others. I initially welcomed their critical appraisal because, while I didn't agree with all of it, I agreed that opening up discussion was a good thing to do. However, when I saw how conservative journalists and anti-feminist critics weaponised their paper to argue that Our Watch was "gender-biased" and that violence against women had nothing to do with gender, I became concerned about the unintended effect of the paper. In my response to *Losing It*, I want to focus on two issues that I think warrant a deeper analysis: the "Nordic paradox" and the issue of gendered drivers and reinforcing factors.

During the 1970s and 1980s, there was recognition among feminist academics and activists that patriarchy was the major cause of violence against women. There was pushback, primarily from men, to the concept of patriarchy, so the language of gender inequality was used instead. The promotion of gender equality is premised on the view that a lack of it is a major driver of violence against women.

I believe we need to bring back "patriarchy" into the lexicon to explain why men's violence against women persists and why attempts to address it have not been successful over the last fifty years. A nuanced concept of patriarchy accounts for men's structural power over women and the deeply embedded patriarchal sense of self experienced by many men. Gender inequality, usually framed by neo-liberal economic indicators, does not capture that complexity. Here, the so-called Nordic paradox is revealing.

Until recently, there has been no acknowledgement by violence prevention advocates in Australia that there are high levels of violence against women in the Nordic countries. These countries are presented as being gender-equal when compared to other countries around the globe. However, the levels of violence against women in Nordic countries do not constitute a paradox. The measures of gender equality used in these countries are based primarily on the distribution of material goods and economic power. These measures do not address the traditional gendered division of labour in the private sphere. Less attention is given to the cultural domination of men and masculinity over women and femininity, and to women's primary responsibility for domestic work and childcare. So these public gender equality measures in the Nordic countries did not address the daily interaction between men and women. In fact, the Nordic countries are not as gender-equal as they are believed to be. Because of the deeply internalised misogyny, sexism and sense of male entitlement among many Nordic men, these men are likely to resist greater gender equality in the public realm and many will use violence against women as one expression of their perceived lack of power. This is sometimes referred to as "the backlash thesis." So in the Nordic countries, patriarchal power persists in the context of progressive gender equality policies.

Some anti-feminist commentators and academics have used the Nordic paradox to undermine feminist analyses more widely and argue that gender-neutral approaches that focus on men's socioeconomic vulnerability, mental ill-health, trauma, use of alcohol, stress and exposure to violence should be given more attention. This leads to the second issue that I want to comment on: gendered drivers and reinforcing factors.

Jess Hill notes that *Change the Story* arranged risk factors in a hierarchy, whereby "gendered drivers," such as condoning of violence against women, men's control of decision-making, rigid gender roles and male peer relations, were seen as more significant than "reinforcing factors," such as mental illness, trauma, alcohol use and exposure to violence. Our Watch gives priority to the gendered drivers. However, in my view, the four gendered drivers are themselves simply manifestations of the wider problem of patriarchy. Addressing these gendered drivers will not necessarily challenge patriarchy, any more than addressing the reinforcing factors will bring about significant change. This is because the gendered drivers do not address either the structural dimensions of patriarchy or the deeply embedded patriarchal subjectivities of men. To claim otherwise is to engage in a form of cruel optimism, where unrealistic expectations are espoused that are unable to be achieved without significant structural and cultural change.

Hill argues that Our Watch, in giving greater attention to some risk factors than others, is pursuing a "narrow" prevention strategy. Various advocates for other factors, such as child maltreatment, attachment issues, trauma and alcohol, are given voice in the Quarterly Essay to emphasise their importance to violence prevention. The debate is framed as the "feminist model" versus the "psychopathology model" and the proposed solution is to integrate both models. I would like to suggest a different way of approaching this conflict. I argue that we should bring a gendered analysis to the so-called reinforcing factors.

By way of example, socioeconomic vulnerability undermines men's capacity to exercise particular forms of masculinity, and violence is one way to restore a sense of manhood for men. Alcohol use frees up any inhibitions men might feel about using violence to coerce their partners. Men whose expectations about manhood are about being strong, in control and stoic will experience trauma and feeling out of control as a threat to their masculinity, and again, violence is one response to their anger and rage. So in my view, these other factors are not in tension with a gendered analysis but rather are part of that analysis.

Having said that, these issues, which Michael Salter calls the "inner world" of men, are not so amenable to population-based violence prevention policies. Rather, many of them require face-to-face, feminist-informed engagement with men. This engagement, however, should be connected with policies addressing the wider patriarchal context to avoid individualised solutions to what is a socio-political problem. Until we understand the multiplicity of ways in which patriarchy is perpetuated by governments, private corporations and men in general, we will not address the fundamental causes of men's violence and misogyny. It is time to deepen the gender analysis, not to weaken it or to step back from it.

Bob Pease

LOSING IT

Response to Correspondence

Jess Hill

I am grateful to all who took the time to engage with my essay. Ever since I began writing on family, domestic and sexual violence, I've been navigating the significant differences of opinion among experts across Australia on how best to prevent gendered violence. That diversity of perspective is evident not only in the essay itself but also among the leading voices published in this correspondence. I hope this Quarterly Essay will help the various parties working to reduce gendered violence to engage with each other in genuine curiosity and openness. As Professor Enrique Gracia (the Spanish co-author of the 2016 Nordic paradox paper) points out, the persistently high rates of gendered violence among young people across the world (including Australia) highlight that, right now, "the problem, hidden in plain sight – is that we don't know how to prevent it." This should inspire a degree of humility in all of us.

Professor Salter writes that *Losing It* "is a klaxon call for accountability – not only for the men who perpetrate violence, or those who enable it, but for the publicly funded prevention organisations and professionals tasked with protecting the community." All of us working to end gendered violence – and I include myself here – are accountable for our actions and commitments. For this, there is a simple reference point: the level of violence against women and children. It is indisputable that, despite unprecedented investment in prevention, gendered violence is not going down, and that in some areas (especially tech surveillance, image-based abuse and youth-on-youth sexual assault) it is even increasing. This is the grim reality that the Quarterly Essay seeks to grapple with. I note that some of my interlocutors hold this at front of mind, but not all.

Marcia Neave, who was the chair of the landmark Victorian Royal Commission into Family Violence, questions "the apparent lack of influence of the Victorian royal commission on the initial development of a national prevention strategy." Last year, I was appointed to the Commonwealth's Rapid Review into Prevention, which Neave describes as "a more nuanced approach" that more faithfully represents the commission's findings – that critical points of prevention exist at every point of contact.

Ultimately, Neave and I are in lockstep on the best way forward: "The main hope for change lies in experimenting with new approaches, collecting data and evaluating the evidence about what works and what approaches should be abandoned because they are ineffective." This is the kind of openness, transparency and flexibility the essay is calling for.

Neave asks why "it has taken so long to recognise the limitations of a strategy which places most of its eggs in the basket of addressing gender inequality." My first critique of the gender equality approach to prevention appeared in *See What You Made Me Do* in 2019, with on-record support from Professor Michael Salter. We communicated our critique directly to Our Watch's CEO, Patty Kinnersly, in a private meeting at the time; colleagues across the sector who shared these misgivings discussed them in private. However, before and after 2019, those who openly questioned the dominant prevention model were often misrepresented, which had – and continues to have – a chilling effect on open, honest and necessary debate. As Anne Manne writes, rigid adherence to the dominant paradigm, "aggressively patrolled ... is rarely helpful in bending the arc towards justice."

This pattern of misrepresentation and groupthink is apparent in less charitable responses to the essay. There is an extraordinary admission from Kelleher et al. that best summarises the echo chamber they occupy when they write: "Open and honest debate, as Hill calls for on these factors or other prevention approaches, is not how knowledge is advanced." Why? "Because debate is often loaded with ideology rather than the best evidence available, or with the noisiest and sometimes least informed voices." This letter, drafted by two Victorian consultants who have received funding from Our Watch, and the CEO of a Victorian women's health service, encapsulates the unhealthy degree of insulation from scrutiny and public accountability that has developed in some areas of prevention work. It is a far cry from the call of the head of Women's Community Shelters, Annabelle Daniel, who in the essay insists: "This literally has as the endpoint the lives of women and children. It is a critical conversation that we have to have. And what we can't let get in the way is organisational ego, research ego, or organisational self-perpetuation, or more funding, or any of those things. Our eye has to be on solving the problem."

If not through "open and honest debate," how should knowledge of primary prevention best be advanced? Around the private boardroom tables of Victorian prevention agencies? In closed rooms with Chatham House rules? Should we apply the same ethos to other matters of national significance? And if such conversations happened only in private, what would move those with a vested interest in the status quo to consider contradictory evidence?

On the subject of transparency, I was very pleased to see a response to the essay from Patty Kinnersly. However, Kinnersly repeats the same argument she made when Professor Salter and I met her in 2019, when she warned us that it was not the right time to speak publicly about our misgivings about her organisation's approach. Today, she again insists that "this social context means now is not the time to reduce the focus on gender equality and the rights of women – one of the foundation stones of Australia's prevention efforts." This is a stark misrepresentation of my position and my essay. I have never argued that we should reduce our national focus on gender equality. My point, readily understood by other correspondents, is that the narrow focus on gender equality has seen other key areas of prevention neglected in practice. Making this point does not, as Kinnersly implies, make me anti-feminist or opposed to the advance of women's rights. My concerns are shared in these pages by Professor Anne Summers, who is not only one of the most prominent and longstanding advocates for gender equality in Australia but also the co-founder of Elsie's, Australia's first domestic violence refuge. Is Summers anti-feminist when she notes the shortcomings of this approach to prevention?

Kinnersly says it is "demonstrably false" to suggest that Our Watch has ignored alcohol, gambling and childhood trauma. Leading advocates in these areas disagree. National Children's Commissioner Anne Hollonds says, "Children are the prevention opportunity that has been ignored." Leading expert on child abuse and gendered violence Cathy Humphreys says that, while alcohol's role in domestic violence is a "national emergency," there has been "silence in this area." Kinnersly makes strong statements about "the evidence" and "what works." However, Professor Salter has gone on the record numerous times now, including in his response to this essay, about the rejection of evidence he provided on poverty and alcohol for the original literature review for *Change the Story* as early as 2014. These issues have been subordinated in the Our Watch frameworks, and are largely (if not entirely) absent from the agency's advocacy. As Salter remarks, "In violence prevention, what matters is not what appears in a well-designed report, but what is prioritised, resourced and embedded in practice." Kinnersly points out that *Change the Story* was "updated based on over 500 pieces of new evidence." But the length of a bibliography in a policy document does not prove that the strategies it contains are working. In her correspondence, Anne Manne states a simple truth: "*Whatever works.* That has to be the simple benchmark for assessing the effectiveness of the nation's response to violence against women and children."

I was happy, as always, to read correspondence from Bob Pease, a pioneer in the area of gendered violence, who was a key early influence on my work. I concur with Pease's assessment that patriarchy is the deep, sociological grid in which all human relationships and systems – law, government, education, military and health – play out. Ideally, all prevention strategies would be grounded in an awareness of patriarchy, of which (as Pease points out) gender inequality is one symptom. Pease's analysis of patriarchy is important as a root cause. However, it's one thing to identify the cause, quite another to find a set of solutions to it. Pease says that a prevention model that falls short of addressing the structural dimensions of patriarchy is engaging in "a form of cruel optimism."

But is it not also "cruel optimism" to depend on the overthrow of patriarchy to achieve tangible reductions in gendered violence? The fact remains that, right now, our society is boiling with the impact of deeply engrained patriarchal responses that have passed through multiple generations. As I point out in the essay, "prevention work has to find a way into the minds and bodies of those who are most likely to act violently … and persuade them not to do so." We need to identify ways to do this *within* a patriarchal society – one that we cannot realistically expect to be radically restructured any time soon. I would also contest the notion that "the levels of violence against women in Nordic countries do not constitute a paradox," because Nordic countries are rated highly on structural gender equality, a measure that doesn't include factors like the gendered division of domestic labour. A cursory look at statistics from Sweden, for example, shows that the gendered division of household labour is more equal than the European average. I agree we have not yet properly understood why rates of violence in Nordic countries are so high, but the paradox cannot be dismissed (despite the concerted efforts of many academics over the past decade). It's for this reason that the Swedish government itself has commissioned further research on it.

There is a welcome focus on childhood trauma and the complexity of the lives of violent men from Russell Marks. I understand Marks' frustration. He is working at the coalface as a lawyer in the Northern Territory and sees the grim consequences of systems failure and inadequacy up close. While I have great sympathy for his position, I am not a suitable avatar for his frustrations. Many of the points that Marks makes – especially about the nefarious impact of systems, the inner worlds of men who use violence and control, the frustration over a narrow conception of what drives that violence – have long been central to my work. I've explored the various ways in which childhood trauma, including emotional abuse and toxic shaming, have contributed to the dynamics of power and control in men's intimate relationships at great length and in the spirit of "compassionate accountability" modelled by prevention organisations such as She Is Not Your Rehab. My centring of trauma as a prominent background factor to men's violence is not a recent conversion "at long last" to "the facts," as Marks asserts. Neither is the domestic violence sector blind to the many issues he raises, particularly that of victim misidentification, and how the combined racism and misogyny of some police result in Aboriginal victim-survivors especially being misidentified as perpetrators, with some ending up jailed as a result and their children removed.

Though Marks claims to have read my book, he somehow manages to completely misrepresent it. I did not, as Marks claims, essentialise domestic violence offenders as "cobras" or "pitbulls"; I described the various ways in which researchers, *including* Gottman and Jacobson (of the infamous cobras/pitbulls typology), have attempted to distil the chaos of abusive behaviour into clear, observable patterns. To the men I interviewed who had used coercive control I never assigned such labels.

He neglects also to mention the entire chapter on the connection between shame and violence (particularly the notion of "humiliated fury") that I co-wrote with my partner, David Hollier, who works in private practice as a psychotherapist. In this chapter, we sought to complicate the narrative of how power-and-control sits behind men's violence: "There is often a big difference between how powerful abusers *look* and how powerful they *feel*," we wrote. "This, I believe, is one of the major elements missing from the mainstream understanding of domestic abuse: the fact that in the moments before a man takes control, he can feel at his most vulnerable and powerless, just milliseconds before feeling the flush of power and pride that comes from reinstating dominance." This analysis was developed further in my 2021 podcast series *The Trap*, produced with the Victorian Women's Trust, in which the backgrounds of abusive men were explored in greater detail, including an interview with Maggie Woodhead, who worked with some of the most hardcore offenders in Western Australian prisoners, and found that among the cohort she was working with, 86 per cent had grown up with domestic abuse. As I concluded in this episode, "In refusing to talk openly about the role of men's trauma, we're simply reinforcing the same old patriarchal culture: as the great bell hooks writes, this is 'one that socialises men to deny their feelings and in which male pain can have no voice, and male hurt cannot be named or healed.' When we frame abusive men simply as powerful and privileged, we neglect what hooks calls 'the deep inner misery of men … the terrible terror that gnaws at the soul when one cannot love.'"

Marks makes other sweeping claims about the criminalisation of coercive control – an important area of my work – that are simply incorrect. While he argues that coercive control laws have been "achieved across the country," they have in fact only been legislated in two states – New South Wales and Queensland – and operationalised only in New South Wales since July last year. Other states and territories, including South Australia, Western Australia and the ACT, are still in the process of drafting legislation. In effect for less than a year in one state, and Marks is already confident enough to declare the laws have failed. He also doesn't mention the multi-sector education, capacity-building and response efforts on coercive control that have gained momentum since the laws were introduced and are already improving the safety of women and children. The expanded definition of domestic violence that he sees in his work at the civil level – regarding the issuing of intervention orders – has been in the Territory's *Domestic Violence Act* since 2007 and has nothing to do with more recent debates on coercive control laws. Additionally, in his critique of the sector's supposedly "pro-carceral" position (a moniker many across the sector would baulk at, and one I do not identify with, having advocated strongly for alternative responses such as justice reinvestment), he offers no answer to the question that confronts frontline services and first responders every day: what should we do about violent, controlling and fixated men once they are maiming, raping and threatening the lives of women and children? How do we right now protect women and children from men who are intent on murdering them? The safety of women and children who face such violence barely warrants a mention in Marks' correspondence.

I am grateful as always for the contribution of Manjula O'Connor, who is one of the most accomplished thinkers on gendered violence in Australia, particularly its impact on South Asian women and children. Her incisive analysis of coercive control, which is commonly perpetrated also by extended family members (the power residing most forcefully in many cases with the mother-in-law) and perpetuated by the state, requires greater attention from policymakers and legislators. It was a privilege to present alongside O'Connor to the South Australian parliament on the care and consideration that must be taken if coercive control laws are introduced in that state.

Finally, I am honoured also to do this work alongside the esteemed Dr Anne Summers, whose pioneering work over many decades has fundamentally changed Australia for the better. Her contribution to these pages stands on its own; I wish only to echo her urgent frustration over the fundamental failure of policymakers to treat this issue with the seriousness it requires.

Several correspondents bemoaned the lack of attention given to gendered violence during the election campaign. I'm not so bothered by that, because the promise has already been made. Federal, state and territory governments have all committed to end gendered violence within a single generation, but they have not yet grasped the gravity of their own promise and how their approach must radically improve to meet this challenge. That's not something they need to prosecute during an election campaign – the mandate is already there. In its election-day editorial, *The Sydney Morning Herald* too bemoaned the lack of focus on gendered violence. That is welcome, but why don't outlets such as the *Herald* put their money where their mouth is and hire dedicated reporters to focus on this area? Why don't think-tanks like the Australia and Grattan institutes focus on this as an important area of policy? Governments get away with tinkering around the edges because they face so little pressure on this issue, except from the feminist sector, which is responding to an ever-escalating crisis of violence and has precious little time to advocate. To all who fail to step up to this cause, I reiterate Summers' closing words: "They won't be able to say they weren't warned."

Jess Hill

Marilyn Beaumont was CEO of Women's Health Victoria from 1995 to 2010.

Jess Hill is an investigative journalist and the author of *See What You Made Me Do* and two Quarterly Essays, *The Reckoning* and *Losing It*. She has presented two highly acclaimed docuseries on SBS and a podcast titled *The Trap*. Her work has won three Walkley Awards, an Amnesty International Award and the Stella Prize in 2020.

Helen Keleher is a professor, and was lead researcher and writer for *Change the Story: Australia's National Framework for the Prevention of Violence Against Women and Children*.

Patty Kinnersly is CEO of the primary prevention organisation Our Watch.

Anne Manne is a regular contributor to *The Age* and *The Monthly*. Her books include *Crimes of the Cross*, *The Life of I*, *Motherhood* and the Quarterly Essay *Love & Money*.

Russell Marks is a criminal defence lawyer and the author of *Crime and Punishment* and *Black Lives, White Law*.

Marcia Neave retired from the bench of the Victorian Supreme Court in 2014 to become commissioner of the Royal Commission into Family Violence in Victoria.

Manjula Datta O'Connor is a psychiatrist in private practice, a founding director of the AustralAsian Centre for Human Rights and Health and the author of *Daughters of Durga*.

Bob Pease was a founding member of Men Against Sexual Assault in Melbourne, and his books include *Facing Patriarchy* and *Undoing Privilege*.

Michael Salter is a professor of criminology and director of the Childlight East Asia and Pacific Hub, University of New South Wales.

Anne Summers is a journalist and the author of nine books, including the classic *Damned Whores and God's Police*. She is currently Professor of Domestic and Family Violence at the Business School at UTS.

Hugh White is the author of *The China Choice* and *How to Defend Australia*, and three previous Quarterly Essays, *Power Shift*, *Without America* and *Sleepwalk to War*. He is emeritus professor of strategic studies at ANU and was the principal author of Australia's Defence White Paper 2000.

QUARTERLY ESSAY BACK ISSUES

- ☐ **QE 1** *In Denial* by Robert Manne $27.99
- ☐ **QE 2** *Appeasing Jakarta* by John Birmingham $27.99
- ☐ **QE 3** *The Opportunist* by Guy Rundle $27.99
- ☐ **QE 4** *Rabbit Syndrome* by Don Watson $27.99
- ☐ **QE 5** *Girt By Sea* by Mungo MacCallum $27.99
- ☐ **QE 6** *Beyond Belief* by John Button $27.99
- ☐ **QE 7** *Paradise Betrayed* by John Martinkus $27.99
- **QE 8** *Groundswell* by Amanda Lohrey OUT OF STOCK
- ☐ **QE 9** *Beautiful Lies* by Tim Flannery $27.99
- ☐ **QE 10** *Bad Company* by Gideon Haigh $27.99
- ☐ **QE 11** *Whitefella Jump Up* by Germaine Greer $27.99
- ☐ **QE 12** *Made in England* by David Malouf $27.99
- ☐ **QE 13** *Sending Them Home* by Robert Manne with David Corlett $27.99
- ☐ **QE 14** *Mission Impossible* by Paul McGeough $27.99
- ☐ **QE 15** *Latham's World* by Margaret Simons $27.99
- ☐ **QE 16** *Breach of Trust* by Raimond Gaita $27.99
- ☐ **QE 17** *'Kangaroo Court'* by John Hirst $27.99
- ☐ **QE 18** *The Worried Well* by Gail Bell $27.99
- ☐ **QE 19** *Relaxed & Comfortable* by Judith Brett $27.99
- ☐ **QE 20** *A Time for War* by John Birmingham $27.99
- ☐ **QE 21** *What's Left? by Clive Hamilton* $27.99
- ☐ **QE 22** *Voting for Jesus* by Amanda Lohrey $27.99
- ☐ **QE 23** *The History Question* by Inga Clendinnen $27.99
- ☐ **QE 24** *No Fixed Address* by Robyn Davidson $27.99
- ☐ **QE 25** *Bipolar Nation* by Peter Hartcher $27.99
- ☐ **QE 26** *His Master's Voice* by David Marr $27.99
- ☐ **QE 27** *Reaction Time* by Ian Lowe $27.99
- ☐ **QE 28** *Exit Right* by Judith Brett $27.99
- ☐ **QE 29** *Love & Money* by Anne Manne $27.99
- ☐ **QE 30** *Last Drinks* by Paul Toohey $27.99
- ☐ **QE 31** *Now or Never* by Tim Flannery $27.99
- ☐ **QE 32** *American Revolution* by Kate Jennings $27.99
- ☐ **QE 33** *Quarry Vision* by Guy Pearse $27.99
- ☐ **QE 34** *Stop at Nothing* by Annabel Crabb $27.99
- ☐ **QE 35** *Radical Hope* by Noel Pearson $27.99
- ☐ **QE 36** *Australian Story* by Mungo MacCallum $27.99
- ☐ **QE 37** *What's Right?* by Waleed Aly $27.99
- ☐ **QE 38** *Power Trip* by David Marr $27.99
- ☐ **QE 39** *Power Shift* by Hugh White $27.99
- ☐ **QE 40** *Trivial Pursuit* by George Megalogenis $27.99
- ☐ **QE 41** *The Happy Life* by David Malouf $27.99
- ☐ **QE 42** *Fair Share* by Judith Brett $27.99
- ☐ **QE 43** *Bad News* by Robert Manne $27.99
- ☐ **QE 44** *Man-Made World* by Andrew Charlton $27.99
- ☐ **QE 45** *Us and Them* by Anna Krien $27.99
- ☐ **QE 46** *Great Expectations* by Laura Tingle $27.99
- ☐ **QE 47** *Political Animal* by David Marr $27.99
- ☐ **QE 48** *After the Future* by Tim Flannery $27.99
- ☐ **QE 49** *Not Dead Yet* by Mark Latham $27.99
- ☐ **QE 50** *Unfinished Business* by Anna Goldsworthy $27.99
- ☐ **QE 51** *The Prince* by David Marr $27.99
- ☐ **QE 52** *Found in Translation* by Linda Jaivin $27.99
- ☐ **QE 53** *That Sinking Feeling* by Paul Toohey $27.99
- ☐ **QE 54** *Dragon's Tail* by Andrew Charlton $27.99
- ☐ **QE 55** *A Rightful Place* by Noel Pearson $27.99
- ☐ **QE 56** *Clivosaurus* by Guy Rundle $27.99
- ☐ **QE 57** *Dear Life* by Karen Hitchcock $27.99
- ☐ **QE 58** *Blood Year* by David Kilcullen $27.99
- ☐ **QE 59** *Faction Man* by David Marr $27.99
- ☐ **QE 60** *Political Amnesia* by Laura Tingle $27.99
- ☐ **QE 61** *Balancing Act* by George Megalogenis $27.99
- ☐ **QE 62** *Firing Line* by James Brown $27.99
- ☐ **QE 63** *Enemy Within* by Don Watson $27.99
- ☐ **QE 64** *The Australian Dream* by Stan Grant $27.99
- ☐ **QE 65** *The White Queen* by David Marr $27.99
- ☐ **QE 66** *The Long Goodbye* by Anna Krien $27.99
- ☐ **QE 67** *Moral Panic 101* by Benjamin Law $27.99
- ☐ **QE 68** *Without America* by Hugh White $27.99

QUARTERLY ESSAY BACK ISSUES

- ☐ **QE 69** *Moment of Truth* by Mark McKenna $27.99
- ☐ **QE 70** *Dead Right* by Richard Denniss $27.99
- ☐ **QE 71** *Follow the Leader* by Laura Tingle $27.99
- ☐ **QE 72** *Net Loss* by Sebastian Smee $27.99
- ☐ **QE 73** *Australia Fair* by Rebecca Huntley $27.99
- ☐ **QE 74** *The Prosperity Gospel* by Erik Jensen $27.99
- ☐ **QE 75** *Men at Work* by Annabel Crabb $27.99
- ☐ **QE 76** *Red Flag* by Peter Hartcher $27.99
- ☐ **QE 77** *Cry Me a River* by Margaret Simons $27.99
- ☐ **QE 78** *The Coal Curse* by Judith Brett $27.99
- ☐ **QE 79** *The End of Certainty* by Katharine Murphy $27.99
- ☐ **QE 80** *The High Road* by Laura Tingle $27.99
- ☐ **QE 81** *Getting to Zero* by Alan Finkel $27.99
- ☐ **QE 82** *Exit Strategy* by George Megalogenis $27.99
- ☐ **QE 83** *Top Blokes* by Lech Blaine $27.99
- ☐ **QE 84** *The Reckoning* by Jess Hill $27.99
- ☐ **QE 85** *Not Waving, Drowning* by Sarah Krasnostein $27.99
- ☐ **QE 86** *Sleepwalk to War* by Hugh White $27.99
- ☐ **QE 87** *Uncivil Wars* by Waleed Aly & Scott Stephens $27.99
- ☐ **QE 88** *Lone Wolf* by Katharine Murphy $27.99
- ☐ **QE 89** *The Wires That Bind* by Saul Griffith $27.99
- ☐ **QE 90** *Voice of Reason* by Megan Davis $27.99
- ☐ **QE 91** *Lifeboat* by Micheline Lee $27.99
- ☐ **QE 92** *The Great Divide* by Alan Kohler $27.99
- ☐ **QE 93** *Bad Cop* by Lech Blaine $27.99
- ☐ **QE 94** *Highway to Hell* by Joëlle Gergis $27.99
- ☐ **QE 95** *High Noon* by Don Watson $27.99
- ☐ **QE 96** *Minority Report* by George Megalogenis $29.99
- ☐ **QE 97** *Losing It* by Jess Hill $29.99

Order back issues online

Prices include GST.
$10 flat-rate shipping within Australia.
Please include this form with delivery and payment details overleaf.
Back issues also available as ebooks from ebook retailers.